BEYOND THE STRINGS

BEYOND
THE STRINGS

BECOMING A LEADER THAT GENERATES THE MIRACULOUS AND DITCHES THE RULES.

TOMMY WAFFORD

Clear Wind
PUBLISHING

Beyond The Strings

Clear Wind Publishing

Clear Wind
PUBLISHING

Copyright © 2023 by Tommy Wafford

Library of Congress Cataloging-in-Publication Data is available.

ISBN: 979-8-218-15463-9

TABLE OF CONTENTS

FOREWORD 11

INTRODUCTION 17

MAKING YOUR DREAM A REALITY 20

EXCELLENCE IS ALWAYS A STRATEGY 36

MODEL WHAT YOU WANT 55

GETTING THE WIN THROUGH
PARTNERSHIPS 71

NAVIGATING THE MIRACULOUS 89

ACTIVATING YOUR MIRACLE 105

PROGRESSING YOUR MIRACLE
THROUGH LEADERSHIP 123

PREVENTING MUTINIES 136

COUNTING THE COST OF THE
RISK WORTH TAKING 153

DREAMS REALLY DO COME TRUE 165

To Kelly, Jackson, Elliot, and Sutton.
Thank you for letting me lead.

"ONE DAY, YOU WILL BE OLD ENOUGH TO START READING FAIRYTALES AGAIN."

C.S. LEWIS

LEARN LIKE A KID.
LEAD LIKE A GROWNUP.

By: Dave Willis

I'm pretty old. I'm not ancient, but I'm old enough to have plenty of gray hairs and old enough to think the music is usually too loud. I've learned a lot of lessons with age, and one of the most important lessons is in realizing how much more I still have to learn.

Instead of growing into a rigid, closed-minded old man, I want to keep learning. I want to hold onto childlike wonder. I want to rediscover the beautiful lessons in children's stories and be reminded that the most profound truths are often hidden in unexpected places.

I'm a dad of four sons. Two of them are already teenagers and two of them are in elementary school. This basically means that two of my kids still think I'm cool and the two older ones have figured out that I'm definitely not cool. With a house full of boys, we've had our share of broken glasses and broken bones, but we have a lot of fun. When our youngest son was five years old, his imaginative spirit almost burned our house down during a dinner party. Seriously. Here's what happened…

We were having some friends over for dinner and my amazing wife, Ashley, had the entire house looking and smelling perfect. She lit a scented candle in our bathroom and then the candle was placed inside a decorative metal cylinder which gave a lovely glow to the room. The candle also helped disguise some of the nasty smells that can fill our bathroom. One of our guests walked into the bathroom and shouted out, "Wow! There's a huge fire in here!"

We rushed into the bathroom and the metal cylinder with the scented candle inside was shooting out flames like it was a blow torch! We frantically carried the flaming cylinder outside and threw water on it until it stopped. Our neighbors probably thought we were crazy and having a bonfire on our front yard in the middle of winter.

We came back in the house and started trying to figure out what had caused the fire. We asked the kids if anyone had done anything to the candle and our five-year-old slowly raised his hand with a look of shame and embarrassment on his face. We asked him what happened, and he said he had been throwing toilet paper into the metal cylinder to watch the fire burn brighter.

With some firmness and frustration in my voice, I said, "Buddy, that wasn't a good choice. When we're outside together at the fire pit, you can put wood and sticks in the fire as long as I'm there with you, but we never ever put something on a candle inside a house because it could burn the house down."

He looked at me with a quivering lip and an innocence in his voice when he said, "But daddy, you never teached me that before."

He was right (even though grammatically speaking "teached" isn't a real word). I had never taught him this lesson, so he was trying to figure out the rules about fire on his own. Thankfully, there was no serious damage and he'll remember the lesson the next time he's tempted to throw toilet paper on an open flame.

We've all made mistakes in life. Some of those mistakes are costlier than others. The key is to not repeat mistakes. When we can learn from our own past failures, or even better, learn from the mistakes others have made without making them ourselves, then our lives and leadership will thrive. For that to happen, we must remain humble enough to always keep learning.

If you're reading this book, you're likely already a leader, but you still have more to learn. We all do! There are still things we've never been taught or perhaps some important lessons that we've simply forgotten along the way and need to relearn.

The book you're about to read is a Master Class in leadership development written by a great friend of mine. Tommy Wafford is a leader, entrepreneur, innovator, philanthropist, husband, dad, and man of faith and integrity. I've known him at his lowest points, and I've also known him in seasons of great success. Through it all, he's remained a steadfast example of tenacious grit and unstoppable growth.

Tommy's story is an inspiring journey. He has achieved nearly every aspect of success an entrepreneur could ever hope to gain, but Tommy isn't satisfied with his own success. He wants to make others successful too. He wants to help each leader reach their full potential. That's the heart behind this book.

This book will reintroduce you to a children's story you most likely know from your own childhood. Like many classic children's stories, the story of Pinocchio is rich with life lessons and practical principles. Tommy has unearthed a treasure trove of life and leadership lessons in this beloved story, and he weaves those profound lessons through the tale of his own remarkable journey of life and leadership. The end result is a leadership book unlike any other which is simultaneously wildly entertaining, profoundly practical and deeply inspirational.

I'm so excited for you to begin this journey! I had the privilege of reading this book before it was available to the public, so I know first-hand how impactful this book can be. If you'll apply the principles on the coming pages, your life will improve, and your leadership influence will increase.

You've made such a wise investment by choosing to read this book. I believe it will create immediate value and lifelong impact in your life and your career. I believe your childlike wonder is about to be reawakened and your capacity for growth is about to expand exponentially. A great adventure is in store for you! I'm cheering you on as you begin.

Dave Willis
Author, Pastor, Podcaster and Lifelong Learner

INTRODUCTION

I never set out to be an entrepreneur, and I'm not really sure if I knew what an entrepreneur was until I became one. The idea never crossed my mind until the day I was fired from a job where I was successful at leading, but bad at managing. Angry, resentful, and uncertain of my next step, I realized I needed to take control of my future and be the captain of my ship. I was done working for someone else, and I knew I would rather work 100 hours a week for myself than 40 hours a week for someone else.

I took control of an emotional situation, but for others, it's an opportunity to create a better life for themselves that drives them to entrepreneurship. The meaning—or the why—behind becoming an entrepreneur is deeply personal. If you are endeavoring to be an entrepreneur and don't have a personal reason for doing so, there's a high likelihood you will fail. You won't fail because you aren't skilled enough or prepared enough or even resourced enough. You'll fail because it's indescribably difficult to do. There will be countless moments where it will feel like the whole house is on fire, and without something deeply personal to save, you'll sit outside wishing for the fire department to respond faster instead of running back into the flames, braving the smoke and the danger, to save the last little bit of meaning left so you can rebuild again and again.

Being an entrepreneur means you want to run a business because you're crazy enough to believe you can. Some people get to realize that dream, and some people only want to do it but never see it happen. The difference between the "getters" and "wanters" is the amount of leadership it takes to get there. And everything in life comes down to leadership. As an entrepreneur, you are constantly trying to be both the leader you always wish you worked for and the employee you always wish worked for you. Entrepreneurship is a unique opportunity to take an inventory of the faults and failures you may have as both. If you can correct them when it is just you, or just you and a few people, then your odds for success increase. But if not, well, the house will burn.

Sometimes we won't know what is in us until we face a crisis (our proverbial burning house), and we decide whether the crisis will launch our dream or kill it. My crisis launched me into a life I could never have imagined and one I would never want to change. After 15 years as an entrepreneur and successful business owner, I've discovered everything in life and in business is won or lost in one word—leadership.

THE DIFFERENCE BETWEEN THE **GETTERS** AND **WANTERS** IS THE AMOUNT OF LEADERSHIP IT TAKES TO GET THERE. AND EVERYTHING IN LIFE COMES DOWN TO LEADERSHIP.

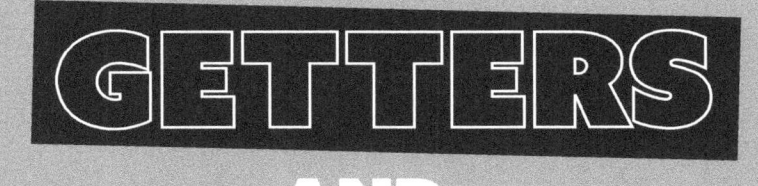

Chapter One

MAKING YOUR DREAM A REALITY

PINOCCHIO'S TRAGEDY

One night, I woke up from a dead sleep with the weirdest thought. I said out loud into the dark, "Pinocchio is such a tragedy." As I lay there trying to go back to sleep, I couldn't get the story of Pinocchio out of my head. I was struck by the thought that Pinocchio is an awful tragedy. Maybe you have never connected Walt Disney's rendition of Pinocchio as a tragedy. I know I never did.

Pinocchio is a tragedy for one incredibly simple reason: He desperately wanted to be a "real boy" instead of realizing the supernatural phenomenon that he was. He was a talking pile of sticks, after all. But the more I processed this thought, the more I understood the story of Pinocchio is both a metaphor and a cautionary tale for successful leaders.

Consider Geppetto for a moment. He had an impossible dream—or at least to him it seemed impossible. Geppetto was a talented man. He was a single, local small business owner who had a shop where he made artisan woodcraft by hand. Not to mention, he had shaggy hair and an awesome mustache. If he lived in the new "hipster" Brooklyn, he would have been the most eligible bachelor on his block and yet, he was alone—just him, his cat, and his goldfish.

Geppetto spent his days and evenings carving because, as a business owner, that's what you do. You work until the work is done and then you work some more. But in reality, we only know one key detail about Geppetto. With one peek into the man behind the woodworking, we discover he has a singular dream. Geppetto's dream is to have a son. We are left to infer most of the other details about Geppetto's life. We know he doesn't have a wife, and there are no signs that he's on the market or searching for a suitable mate.

He might not have been able to get married because of his poor circumstances. He may have had a family that was tragically ripped from him through an unfortunate set of circumstances. Maybe he has a crippling fear of girls and is some sort of wood-carving recluse that pines over the bachelorettes who purchase tables and chairs for their dowries but will never belong to him. Maybe he sees his own mortality approaching, and without a son to carry on his woodworking, he would be left destitute and starving. Honestly, who knows?

HE DESPERATELY WANTED TO BE A "REAL BOY" INSTEAD OF REALIZING THE SUPERNATURAL PHENOMENON THAT HE WAS.

What I think is interesting about Geppetto's dream is that it seems like he is not taking the traditional route to accomplishing it. That leaves a lot of questions unanswered. Why isn't he on Tinder or Bumble or Seeking Arrangements, for that matter? Why has he abandoned the old-fashioned tried-and-true methods of finding a mate? Geppetto's dream isn't even that crazy a dream. Hundreds, maybe even thousands, of other villagers have solved the procreation puzzle. Why can't Geppetto? What is his particular hurdle to success? Is he lazy? Preoccupied with his business? Insecure about his skills with the ladies? What we know for certain is, he's missing the prerequisite partner to make it happen. Geppetto's dream is impossible for him to accomplish by himself.

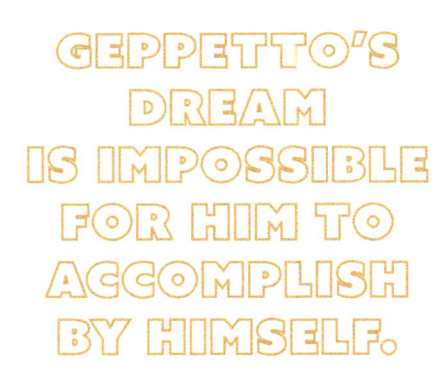

GEPPETTO'S DREAM IS IMPOSSIBLE FOR HIM TO ACCOMPLISH BY HIMSELF.

It is in Geppetto's inability to produce his dream that I find a connection with the story. I would love to say that I connect with Geppetto's successful career, doing what he loves, or even in his longevity as an entrepreneur. It would make for a wonderful rush for my ego if I could say that I don't identify with people who can't seem to make life or business work for them. But I would be lying. Today, I'm more capable than when I started my business journey, but I learned every lesson the hard way. That's where I connect most with Geppetto—in the struggle.

THE EARLY DAYS

Years ago, I was in a dark place. I had just been let go from a job I loved with very little explanation, other than to say I had done nothing wrong. I had very few prospects for employment in my community, and I had determined that I didn't want to leave the city my wife and I called home. To continue the career path I was on would almost certainly mean a move out of town and maybe out of state, but I had a one-year-old at home, our parents had just moved to be closer to us, and I was burned out on working for someone else.

I always wanted to launch out on my own, but I never had the guts to try it. One of my best friends, Andrew Duke, sat down with me one day and asked what my plan was—I didn't have one. But I mentioned my idea for an app that would allow small businesses to advertise in a unique way and drive traffic into their stores. We hatched a very under-thought plan over a few evening coffee-runs to Starbucks. After picking an incredibly dumb name for the business, I designed a logo in about 20 minutes, and we were ready to order business cards. Andrew and I have been business partners ever since. Like Geppetto, I had a dream I couldn't accomplish on my own. It took a strategic partnership to make our collective dreams happen. It was difficult, and none of what has been accomplished in a relatively short period would have ever been possible without the tireless work of many people.

It is easy to dismiss a dream as impossible when the obstacles in front of you seem insurmountable. Luckily for Andrew, he had me. What he didn't know then, but definitely knows now, is that I can speak with 100 percent confidence on any subject with no real command of the subject matter. So when we first started, nothing seemed like obstacles to me. I would just talk our way around them. It would've been easier to create a list of why we shouldn't start a business, but it was so much more fun pretending we knew what we were doing and solving problems on the fly.

I won't pretend that a partnership is the silver bullet for your dreams, because having a suitable partner for his dream was just one of Geppetto's hurdles, but it is almost always the first step. For me, partnering with Andrew rounded me out without robbing me of my uniqueness. We could see and appreciate the other partner's strengths without rolling our eyes at their shortcomings. We always saw each other as an equal in value, even when we weren't equal in skill.

NO EXCUSE

Geppetto's dream to have a child was going to be hard work, even if he had a suitable partner—the deck was stacked against him. His advanced age and station in life were going to create some interesting challenges. Could he even still have children? But the odds did not deter Geppetto. After looking head on at the obstacles, he held on to his dream. The great divide between "getters" and "wanters" is the ability to see the obstacles and try anyway. Giving up before you start is what most "wantrepreneurs" do.

> **THE GREAT DIVIDE BETWEEN "GETTERS" AND "WANTERS" IS THE ABILITY TO SEE THE OBSTACLES AND TRY ANYWAY.**

The term "wantrepreneur" got popularized in startup circles to describe the people with million-dollar mouths and ten-cent execution. Every networking meetup seems to bring these folks out like the bright blue glow of a bug zapper on a hot summer night.

These pretend pioneers would rather fail with a good excuse than succeed by innovating around the obstacles they face. Their favorite conversations revolve around "what would have been" and how close they once came to success.

One way leaders sabotage themselves is by allowing an excuse to be just that—an excuse. What I mean is that sometimes it is easier to fail with an excuse than it is to succeed, because nowadays it is acceptable to get a participation trophy. You get the dopamine drip of the try, without the win. But the try and the win are not the same. Everybody is not a winner just because they tried. You are only a winner when you win. Don't lower your goal so you can fail with a good excuse.

Geppetto had all the real world excuses anyone could ask for. He could've easily joined a local lonely hearts club and spent the rest of his days playing shuffleboard or backgammon or taking tours of local antique malls, talking about how he would have made an excellent father. He could have bored everyone around him by telling his "I almost got engaged once, but it just didn't work out" story over and over. Geppetto could have even been in "stealth mode," attending speed dating sessions and holding on to the fact that if no one knows what you're hoping for, then no one will know when you failed.

I have attended enough "after-hours, happy hour, brewpub hang, startup-meetup" events to last me for the rest of my life. I'm not saying these events aren't necessary or good for entrepreneurs, because some of us need interaction with the rest of the world (and some sunlight wouldn't kill us either), but real entrepreneurs are in the minority at these events. For the vast majority of the people in attendance, these events are what it means to be an entrepreneur. It really becomes a business lonely hearts club. The same cast of characters is at every meeting. The lady "who would've made an excellent CEO," the "serial entrepreneur" going on and on about how they "almost took an investment once, but

YOUR DEFICIENCIES ARE POWERFUL BECAUSE:

THEY ALERT YOU TO THE OPPORTUNITY FOR A PARTNERSHIP

ALERT YOU TO A PLACE YOU NEED TO BE REFINED

ALERT YOU TO A NEED FOR RESOURCES

REFINE YOUR VISION

AND THEY KEEP YOU CENTERED, HUMBLE AND FUN TO BE AROUND.

it just didn't work out in the end," and of course the "stealth mode" guys. Excuses are the opiate of the entrepreneurial masses, and they are running rampant.

I know it may sound like I have myself together, but really I don't at all. You and I are no different. I've had many excuses for why I didn't accomplish a goal or see a dream become a reality. We all have a ready-made storage container of all our favorite excuses: I'm not connected enough at work. I don't have the prerequisite credentials.

> EVERYBODY IS NOT A WINNER JUST BECAUSE THEY TRIED. YOU ARE ONLY A WINNER WHEN YOU WIN. DON'T LOWER YOUR GOAL SO YOU CAN FAIL WITH A GOOD EXCUSE.

I'm not smart, funny, or attractive enough. But here's what no other book on leadership will tell you—You're right. You are incredibly deficient. Seriously, I don't know of another way to say it. But the good news is, that's okay. You are not meant to be an island. Smart leaders take inventory of not only their strengths but their weaknesses, too. Inventory your deficiencies, and here's why. Your deficiencies are powerful because they alert you to the opportunity for a partnership, alert you to a place you need to be refined, alert you to a need for resources, refine your vision, and keep you centered, humble, and fun to be around.

EXPECT TO ACHIEVE YOUR DREAM

Just like with Geppetto, you will face opposition to your dream, but what you do with the opposition is what will define you as either a leader or a follower. Those who can innovate when they hit barriers are thrust toward their dream. Rarely does anyone accomplish anything of note by themselves. Your dreams, the crazy things you hope for, the things your friends would laugh at you about if they knew you aspired to, are completely out of your reach. So what! What we should learn from is to *still* have the dream.

It's okay to have a dream. It's okay to have this thing you want so badly you can taste it. Even though you can't see a way to do it, it's okay to want it. It's right to still desire this impossible thing, even though you don't know where to begin. Take a note from Geppetto. He never lost hope. Geppetto never gave up, and he did three important things that every successful person does to make their dream become a reality. In the next three chapters, I will show you the Geppetto model of leadership through three principles.

EXCELLENCE IS ALWAYS A STRATEGY.

First, Geppetto kept doing what he was best at. Geppetto knew that excellence is always a strategy. He was clear about where he wanted to be, but not at the expense of where he currently was. Most people think that for them to launch out into a new thing, they have to abandon their current job, position, or responsibilities, but rarely is that the case. The best strategy for the vast majority of people is to continue providing excellent levels of service in their current position. This will probably provide the platform or opportunity for your dream simply because you continued to work with excellence when you didn't have the other components for your dream.

Second, Geppetto used his skills to create a prototype for the future. Geppetto modeled what he wanted, where he was. He could imagine his future son, right down to the clothes he was wearing. Never underestimate the importance of creating a Minimally Viable Version of your dream. You accomplish this by asking, "What is the smallest imaginable version of my dream?" I'm sure Geppetto wasn't creating a marionette as a substitute answer for his dream, but his dream manifested itself in a smaller form through the excellence of his hands. Minimally viable versions create a readiness to seize an opportunity that previously didn't exist.

> **THE BEST STRATEGY FOR THE VAST MAJORITY OF PEOPLE IS TO CONTINUE PROVIDING EXCELLENT LEVELS OF SERVICE IN THEIR CURRENT POSITION.**

Third, Geppetto found strategic partners and let them run with his vision. Geppetto needed help. He was aware he couldn't functionally create a child on his own. He also knew he wasn't participating in any of the time-tested methods of having a child. So he called out for help. Help came in the form of a fairy and a grasshopper. But he never micromanaged their actions. He let them bring their skill sets to the table because the only way to get what he wanted out of life was to give them the freedom to act on his behalf at the moment. He realized big miracles are always facilitated by smaller ones.

ACTIVATE YOUR DREAM

Walt Disney was the greatest storyteller of all time, and he once said that as storytellers, "We restore order with imagination. We instill hope again and again." But what is your story? Better yet, years from now, what do you want your story to be? We know what story Geppetto wanted to tell—what his dream was. He wanted a son. But what about you? What's your dream?

This question might leave you scratching your head, so let me help you out a little bit.

When I help new leaders and entrepreneurs, the first thing I want them to do is to identify their dream. What keeps you up at night? Another question I like to ask that might surprise you is, "What makes you cry? What issues do you notice that you can't stop thinking about?" I believe all of us were born to solve a problem, and that problem is often connected to our dream. Geppetto dreamed of being a dad. I dream of constantly creating something from nothing. What keeps me up at night is the ability to start new things and to create new initiatives. I love to start something that never existed before. At the end of the day, everything comes down to your dream.

The reason it is important to identify your dream is because you have to know what it is you are passionate about. You can be proficient at something without being passionate about it, but that's not excellence. Geppetto knew his dream, and he made his Minimally Viable Version because of it. If you are living life to just survive and get through so you can do what you really want to do, then you are living from the wrong energy. Before you can follow Geppetto's footsteps, you need to identify your dream.

Is there something you dream about doing, but you haven't felt like you could turn it into a lifestyle? Well, you can. Through hard work and never quitting, you can pursue your dream, but like Geppetto, you won't be able to do it alone. You will need others around you like the fairy and the grasshopper to bring your dream to pass. Once you have identified the dream, you have to do the work. I have more seasons than I would like to recount of working 20-hour days.

I've had to shut down businesses and reopen businesses and flip them in a week, and no one was there with me on those lonely 3 a.m. nights. Be willing to be disciplined enough to do the work no one else will do, because that sets entrepreneurs apart. But let me tell you, the effort, the hard work, the failures to get there are all worth it. After you identify your dream, set clear goals for achieving them. "It's not enough to do your best. You must know what to do, and then do your best" (W. Edward Deming). Identify your dream and then move toward it.

WHAT KEEPS YOU UP AT NIGHT? WHAT MAKES YOU CRY? WHAT ISSUES DO YOU NOTICE THAT YOU CAN'T STOP THINKING ABOUT?

THE VISION

As a leader, understand that there is miraculous capacity inside your team and within yourself. You might be a new CEO or entrepreneur, and you know what you want to accomplish, and how you want to do it, but you don't know how to unlock the capacity to accomplish that inside your team members. Throughout this book, I will teach you the things you have to do to qualify yourself for the miraculous.

As you develop as a leader, you will begin to recognize that leadership and management are completely different. A manager knows how to do things right, but a leader knows the right things to do. A manager always depends on the leader for vision, and a leader always depends on the manager for execution. You have to be able to partner with others to achieve your dreams, which is the Geppetto quandary because Geppetto's dream was incomplete without a partner. Geppetto was a visionary without the means of execution. He knew the right things to do; he knew what he wanted to see, but he needed others to execute the vision.

Being the leader doesn't make you better, or somehow higher in status—it just makes you more responsible. You may be an outstanding leader, but it isn't your job as a leader to move the vision along. As the leader, it's your job to write the vision so others can run with it, and this is where partnering with a manager is essential.

When a leader doesn't write the vision for someone else to advance it, then they are like Geppetto, making clocks all day,

BUT A LEADER'S JOB IS TO SET THE BAR AND THEN TO PROTECT THE BAR.

while inventory stockpiles. You may or may not know where you fit in this spectrum yet, but by the end of this book, you will. And regardless of where you fit, the key is that you fit. You have problems to solve, and you have a dream to fulfill, but like Geppetto, you can't do it alone.

EMPOWERED LEADERSHIP

Leadership is two things: empowerment and opportunity. If you have empowered someone and you gave them the opportunity to do it, then you just became a leader. I define empowerment as authority and instruction. Authority is a level of autonomy. If you gave someone authority and you told them how to do it, then you have empowered them. If you look at your organization and you see a large degree of incompetence, what you have is authority with a lack of instruction. On the flip side, if you give team members instruction but no authority, the result is frustration.

Effective leaders empower their team members with the opportunity to complete different tasks with autonomy and clear instructions.

As I interview leaders I often hear stories of moments where they lower the bar so they can get the win. For example, Leader X sets a sales goal for his team, and a couple of days out from their deadline the team is at 50 percent, and it's obvious they aren't going to make it. So Leader X steps in and announces that if they can just get to 75 percent of their goal (a giant compromise), they will still qualify for their incentives, rather than just owning the failure and letting the chips fall where they may. But a leader's job is to set the bar and then to protect the bar. You set the bar by writing your vision and establishing what a clear win looks like.

The leader is responsible for the vision and for what needs to be done to achieve the vision. If you are a leader, the first step in activating your vision is to write it down. Read it daily and share this vision with others.

BLIND CONFIDENCE

Geppetto should be on the entrepreneurial wall of fame, if there was such a thing. Being an entrepreneur is the most nerve-racking thing ever. Every day can feel disoriented and blind and lame and mute simultaneously. No direction you go is right, the speed you're moving is wrong, and nothing you can say makes a difference to anyone around you. I know because I've lived it. However, entrepreneurs all have one thing in common—blind confidence that it will work itself out if they keep hoping and

> HOWEVER, ENTREPRENEURS ALL HAVE ONE THING IN COMMON—BLIND CONFIDENCE THAT IT WILL WORK ITSELF OUT IF THEY KEEP HOPING AND STAY THE COURSE.

stay the course. Even if someone makes a compelling case about how hard it is going to be to raise a child as an impoverished carpenter, you'll just keep hoping. Even if others tell you how dangerous the current climate is to bring up children, you'll just keep hoping. "But what about your work; won't it suffer?" But you will still hope. "What do you know about raising a family?" the crowd scorns, and yet—hope remains.

You get nothing of value that once didn't begin simply as hope, but hope without a strategy is the surest way to breed frustration internally and with those around you. Successful people turn the corner from blind confidence to a defined strategy. You don't have to see the end from the beginning, but you can start, like Geppetto. Clarify your dreams. Add achievable steps to your strategy, and stay the course. Don't waiver or listen to the doubters and the scoffers. Hold on to your crazy dream, and win through strategy and execution—because dreams really do come true.

Chapter Two

EXCELLENCE IS ALWAYS A STRATEGY

The story of Pinocchio opens with the quintessential phrase "One night a long time ago," as a talking cricket introduces us to Geppetto's sleepy village laced with crooked streets where not a soul can be seen. Stars of opportunity shine brightly above the sleepy village where every light is off, save one—Geppetto's. Our narrator, Jiminy Cricket, tells us the only sign of life is Geppetto's shop. While the town's people slumber in apathy, he is hard at work on his passion project—Pinocchio.

Geppetto's ultimate dream is to have a son, and while he doesn't go the traditional route of having one, he knows excellence is always a strategy, so he continues doing what he is best at. Geppetto is clear about where he wants to be, but not at the expense of where he currently is. Most people think that for them to launch out into a new thing, they have to abandon their current job, position, or responsibilities, but rarely is that the case. The best strategy for the vast majority of people is to continue providing excellent levels of service in their current position. Your current position will most likely provide the platform or opportunity for your dream simply because you continued to work with excellence when you didn't have the other components for your dream.

Geppetto understood this, and he worked with excellence on his wood-carving business. He created hundreds of clocks and music boxes with excellence and skill. As Jiminy Cricket walks around Geppetto's shop, he notices the tables are overflowing with Geppetto's handiwork, and the walls were plastered with intricately designed clocks. Geppetto works because there is work to be done. As a result, he is refining his craft so he can ultimately create his dream of having a son.

Geppetto used his skill to create a model of what he wanted in the future. The way this applies to us is that while others are sleeping, so to speak, you stay awake being excellent, and tirelessly working on your passion project. You may dream of starting your own business, creating a new technology, or becoming an executive. No matter the dream, the road to get there is the same for you as it was for Geppetto—excellence. But for you to be excellent in something, you need empathy and proficiency. You can have something be perfect, but if it wasn't done with empathy, then it wasn't excellent. You can do something with passion, but if you didn't have proficiency, then it wasn't excellent, because excellence requires proficiency and empathy.

EXCELLENCE

Are you looking for a career change? Don't know what you should do next? Don't know how to overcome deficiencies with your network or skill sets? Then look at your current position and do that with excellence. Find something about what you do that you can be passionate about, tap into that passion, and perform at the highest possible level. Believe me, you will find out more about yourself in those moments than you ever thought possible.

Empathy and proficiency define excellence, and it is always a strategy for success. What would have happened if Geppetto only worked on clocks, and he never took the time to work on his passion project—his side hustle? If Geppetto had never been working passionately on his side hustle, and being excellent with his job, then he would have missed the miracle when the fairy arrived. In the beginning of Pinocchio, we see thousands of stars hovering over the sleepy town like beacons of opportunity available to everyone, but only one person has a passion project ready for the miraculous to happen. Interestingly, the fairy comes out of the stars and appears in Geppetto's shop. His workplace is the only stop she makes, because he is ready.

How many of us say things like, "Oh, I was going to start that project, but I was too tired," or "Man, I wanted to work on that, but I'm just not feeling like I know the right people"? What would have happened if the fairy arrived and asked Geppetto where the puppet was, and he said, "Oh, I was going to work on that, but I was too sleepy, and I never got to it"? Had he not been working with excellence, then when the time came for the miracle, he would have missed it—he would have nothing for the fairy to use and he would have missed his moment. Geppetto had the same excuses available to all of us, but he didn't use them because his strategy was excellence. But even if it's not your dream—even if it's not what you want—go and do excellent work because excellent work qualifies you for the dream. People want to put opportunity, authority, and responsibility into the hands of someone who will steward them well, and the way you prove to someone you can steward something well is by being excellent with what you have now, because excellence is always a strategy.

Once you identify what you want to do next, it will probably be tied to the same area of passion you discovered in your current role. If you gave that area your best work, you would have a glowing report from your peers and current employer and have grown a competency level with your skill that will make you stand out in your new job. I know I make it sound easy. Believe me, I know from personal experience; it is not. For many of us, it is hard to imagine a correlation between what it is we are able to do with excellence and getting what our heart really desires. Sometimes those things don't seem connected.

In those early days of late nights and no sleep and a startup diet of cheap sandwiches and caffeine, I saw firsthand what it looked like to work with excellence. I wish it was from observing my work, but sadly, that is not the case. Andrew's work ethic was and still is inspiring. He always thought about being on his own as well, and when we launched our company, it was like he was reborn. We joked about the fact that had he been this conscientious an employee in his old job, working for someone else, he would have made everyone look bad. He was a machine. Late in the night, I would have a new idea for a feature, and then I would go out during the day selling our software product to small businesses. But, when I returned, the feature that was just an idea 20 hours ago was done. It amazed me to see an idea spring to life so quickly.

Andrew was so passionate about the experience the user was having on our platform and would deliberate for hours about where a button should go and how we could be better than any of our competitors. He cared about what we were creating together, and it showed through the excellence of his work. Andrew exemplified excellence, and it was infectious. I stepped up my game by learning new skills and performing my job with excellence and passion so I could match his level of competency and pull my weight. The rising tide of Andrew's passion and competency (excellence) lifted all the boats in the harbor—including mine.

EMPATHY

Getting what you want out of life is not complicated. However, even though it is very simple, it is extremely hard to do if you don't have excellence. There are two prerequisites for developing excellence at what you do so you can have whatever it is you want. The first prerequisite is empathy. Developing empathy in your life is essential for achieving your dreams. Passion and empathy are directly connected, and you can't have excellence without them. Joining yourself to someone else's purpose and passion is the definition of empathy. Empathy is what lets you receive what others have done with passion. When someone does something with passion, empathy alerts you to it.

Empathy gives you a window to observe excellence because you see excellence in anything that elicits an emotional response from someone else. When someone has an emotional response to what you have done, then that person has deployed empathy to connect to the thing you wanted them to connect to. Empathy is the receptacle of passion, and it is the ability to see people, products, situations, or ideas through the eyes of others, anticipating what they need. Excellence requires you to identify the principle concern of the person you are trying to empathize with so you can align yourself with them. You are functioning with empathy when you align yourself with someone else. This is what Geppetto did.

If you wanted a clock, you could just get a clock, but Geppetto's clocks were more than that. Geppetto tapped into the needs and interests of his community. He had clocks with wives beating their husbands, children getting spankings, turkeys being butchered, and villagers taking walks. Clock building isn't easy, but Geppetto was a master at making clocks that functioned perfectly. His primitive clocks always fired off at the same time, which is an achievement alone, but even his proficiency wasn't enough. Geppetto needed empathy to connect with his clients. To sell to the butcher, he made

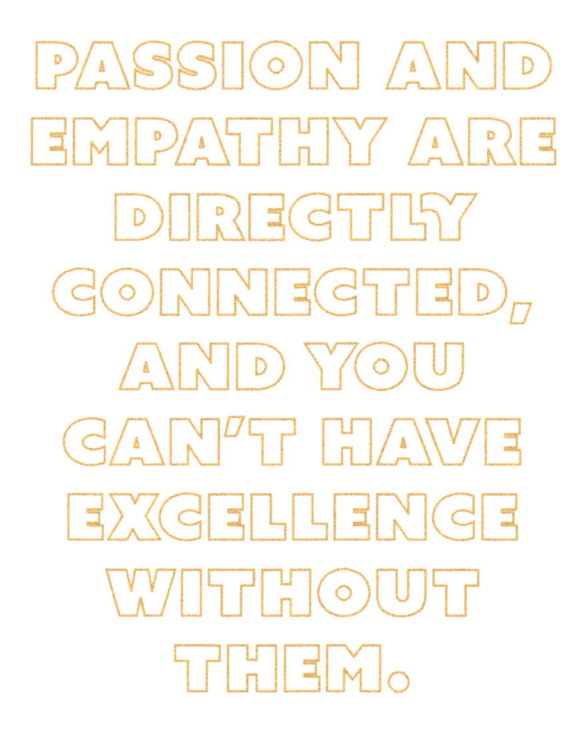

PASSION AND EMPATHY ARE DIRECTLY CONNECTED, AND YOU CAN'T HAVE EXCELLENCE WITHOUT THEM.

the clock with the turkey getting his head lopped off; to sell to the mom with too many kids, he made a clock with kids getting spanked. Geppetto was intimately aware of his community and what spoke to them, so he always tried to find ways to connect with them through his art. Geppetto wanted his art, the thing he was passionate about, to reach his community on their level so they would empathize with him and be moved to buy his product. Excellence means you are attuned to the interests and needs of the recipients of your passion and art.

Imagine if in the opening of Pinocchio, as you entered Geppetto's shop, every clock was identical? What if Geppetto was stubborn about his signature style? What if he said, "This is how I make clocks, and I do it better than anyone else." Imagine you saw hundreds of clocks that were the same, piled up around his shop. What would that say to us? We would think, "No one cares about your signature style. You are busy building something no one wants. Why are you so hardheaded?"

If Geppetto only did what he wanted to do and made clocks he wanted to make, then no one would care. He would be great at making something no one wanted. Thankfully, this is an alternate reality and not the case for our empathic Geppetto. But this is exactly what you do with your life by not being empathetic. A life with no empathy sounds like, "I only want to do it my way. I only want to think about myself. I only want to create for my being." You need empathy to achieve your dreams.

EMPATHY AS STRATEGY

Empathy can also be turned around and used as a strategy. Through my coaching business, I've done sessions with guys who wanted to move their career forward, but they were having trouble getting the attention of their supervisors. Both guys told me what they had done in the last year to increase their department's earnings by 30 percent, engage in other special projects that brought in and trained new people, and completed several extra side projects to shine, but still they weren't being noticed. So I asked each of them, "What's your boss really into? Do they have a favorite sports team? How well do you really know your boss?" Neither understood what I meant, so I explained that in your boss's role, what do you think they care about the most for their job? Does your boss care more about your performance or their own?

It's obvious that your boss is going to care more about their own performance than yours, so you need to ask, "What is my boss getting measured by?" After you determine what they care about for their performance, help them with what is important to their role. Find a way to care about what they care about (empathy), and then, after doing your job well, start doing the things that help your boss look good at their job and that help them win.

Stop doing all the extra things that make you look really good at your job and deploy empathy as a strategy. Find out what is important to your boss, and join them there. Joining yourself to their purpose and passion is how you use empathy as a strategy. If you have time to do an extra project that makes you look good, then you have time to do an extra project that makes your boss look good, because they are the gatekeeper to your future. If you make your supervisor look great, then you will get promoted. In both coaching scenarios, six months later, my clients were promoted, because empathy is a powerful weapon.

When you inspire others and impact their emotional state positively, then you are accessing empathy and utilizing it as a strategy of excellence. For example, if you dream of becoming an executive, then, like Geppetto, use what you have now to create a model for what you want to be in the future. One way you do this is by showing care for people, because that is what executives do. If you want to be an executive one day, then start caring for others today, because excellent leaders show care for others. When leading a team or staff, empathy establishes trust and connectivity. Without empathy, there can be no trust, and the strategy will fail because it hinges on empathy.

How much do you know about the people you work with? How often do you ask them how they are doing or greet them cheerfully? How often does the plight of others drive you to action? Not sure the last time? Well, then you may need a little practice in this area. Still not sure if you have empathy in your life? How often do you give to charitable causes, visit an art gallery, or allow yourself to be moved by music? These types of questions may seem unrelated to excellence, but they are connected. You can't have excellence without empathy, and if you aren't doing the work of keeping your emotional self-pliable and attuned to those you work with and those you work for, then you will not be successful in achieving your dreams.

PRACTICE MAKES PROGRESS

You can practice empathy in two ways: showing care for your team members and peers, and showing care for your boss. Find out what your team members are interested in, if they have kids, what brings them joy, who is their favorite sports team, and what hobbies and interests do they have? Don't stop there. Find out these same details about your boss. Better understanding what makes them tick will help you grow in empathy, and it all starts with being curious.

Being conscientious is another form of empathy. Executives are conscientious about getting their work done because they have shareholders to answer to. Practice being an executive by taking time and care to complete your work on time with excellence. Meeting deadlines, arriving early for work and meetings, and staying until the work is done are all ways you can model being conscientious. And, in the process, you will build trust with those around you.

Spending time thinking about the problem you are trying to solve from an emotional standpoint rather than a technical standpoint also engages empathy. Put yourself in the shoes of the person with the problem and how they feel when they interact with your solution. Ask, "What makes you feel connected to others? What makes me feel connected to the arts? How can I weave that into the experience or reciprocate that feeling?"

For me, I feel the most connected when my experience offers hope. I love music with an "everything is going to be alright" message. I love art that is uplifting and inspirational, and I like people that are convinced that my greatest accomplishments are in front of me, not behind me. Because I have identified what makes me feel most connected to people, I try to emulate that with the people I care about. The more connected to them

PRACTICE BEING AN EXECUTIVE BY TAKING TIME AND CARE TO COMPLETE YOUR WORK ON TIME WITH EXCELLENCE.

I am, the easier it is for me to be passionate about their causes and have them join me in mine. In the things you are in charge of now, build a model in your processes of where you want to be in the future. This is what Geppetto did, and the very thing he had been working on, the wooden puppet, was the very thing that was used to fulfill his dream. You may not be the executive yet, but engaging in empathy today will help you access your dreams tomorrow.

EXCELLENCE IS ONLY PRESENT WHEN THERE IS PASSION AND PROFICIENCY.

PROFICIENCY

The next step toward achieving your goal is developing proficiency. Proficiency or competency is the key to the longevity of your accomplishments. Passion makes them connect, but proficiency makes them stick. Are you familiar with the phrase "Fake it til you make it?" This simply means use your passion until your proficiency catches up. People will overlook a lack of proficiency if the message is delivered with passion. Depending on the product or what you are trying to get people to buy into, there is a timeline of how long they will go with passion over proficiency. Politics is the greatest example of this. Many times, voters have chosen a president with passion who didn't exemplify proficiency. Excellence needs to always be the goal, not proficiency or passion; however, to have excellence, you need both tools.

The journalist Malcolm Gladwell once said, "It takes ten thousand hours to truly master anything. Time spent leads to experience; experience leads to proficiency; and the more proficient you are, the more valuable you'll be." In other words, proficiency will make you more valuable to your supervisor, your organization, and your colleagues. However, it takes time to become proficient in any given area. We see this in Geppetto. While everyone is sleeping, Geppetto is spending countless hours working with wood and carving ornate music boxes and clocks. His light is the last to go out in the village, and most likely it's the first to turn on.

Benjamin Franklin had the same strategy as Geppetto. In his autobiography, Benjamin Franklin explained how, before anyone knew him, one of his strategies to build trust at the beginning of his publishing company was to have the light at his shop be the first everyone noticed in the morning and the last light everyone noticed as they went home for the day. He and Geppetto diligently

ALL WE CAN DO IS TO CONTINUE LOVING OUR DREAM **THE BEST THAT WE CAN; STEWARDING OUR DREAM THE BEST WE CAN STEWARD IT,** AND THEN PUSHING FORWARD WITH EXCELLENCE.

burned the night oil to increase in proficiency so they could do their work with excellence. This is what Andrew and I did in our early years. And when we didn't know how to do something, we wouldn't stop until we learned how and then mastered it, because proficiency requires a high level of competence and skill.

If you aren't sure where you rank on your level of competency and proficiency, then I advise you to try asking your boss. But be forewarned that once you do this, there is no going back. The moment you have a chance for a review, ask your boss, "Hey do you mind if we grab five minutes one day? I have a quick question I want to ask you, but it is a long-term, career-based question, not part of our day-to-day, and I don't want to interrupt your flow."

When the opportunity comes for you to talk to your boss, start with gratitude. Gratitude never hurts, and it always helps. Say something like, "Thanks. I know you have a million things to do and so do I, but thank you for giving me five minutes. I want to know what the one thing is you wish I knew that I currently don't know? What skill do you wish I had that I currently don't have? What level of expertise am I slack on? What is one crucial area that you think I could grow that would be the most beneficial to us as an organization? How can I help to make sure I'm helping you achieve your objectives?" Your boss will answer your question, and then you and improve in that skill or area. Don't just take this question and then do nothing with the answer. Do what your boss tells you to do. This is how you practically increase your proficiency. Once you are clear on the expectation, then fix it, and be ready to engage proficiently.

PIVOT

Excellence is only present when there is passion and proficiency. There is room for improvement if you do something well, but not perfectly. If you do something and the feedback is, "Well, that's good enough," and you don't care, then that means you have run out of passion. If you see you have a lack of proficiency, but a desire to keep going, then you still have passion. And if you reach an adequate level of proficiency but you don't desire to improve, then you have reached the end of your passion and that is the maximum level of excellence you can deliver.

If you get to this point where you realize you have hit one or two roadblocks even though you are proficient and you have been practicing empathy, then your only option is to pivot. Often, when someone pivots, they pivot toward something in their current role where they are proficient or passionate because you can't stay the same. Staying exactly where you are is a slow death, and that isn't what Geppetto did. Geppetto continued to engage the strategy of empathy and proficiency until he saw his dream come to pass.

LEGACY

I am obsessed with the concept of legacy. When anything is done excellently, it becomes transcendent—it transcends time and the space it is in. I know beyond any doubt my greatest contribution to society will be the kids I raise, not the things I do. I want each of my children to grow up to be fully functioning contributors to their world, and this will depend greatly on my competency as a father. Because of that, I am a keen observer of all things fatherhood. When I see dads that are respected by their children as adults, I always ask what advice they would give, because legacy is impossible without competency. Excellence requires that you are good enough at what you create that it will survive your exit.

Geppetto was passionate about his craft. He combined that passion with empathy and a high degree of competency and created excellence. Ultimately, his heart wasn't interested in having an expanded portfolio of clocks on display, and he didn't desire more space for his shop, although he could have used it. In fact, his dream had nothing to do with his trade. He wanted a son. His miracle happened because when it was time for him to get what he wanted most out of life, he had been busy long enough, being excellent that the source materials for his desires were plentiful. Excellence will always open doors without keys, find a way where there are only obstacles, and grow a future out of stagnation.

Geppetto's excellence was the latticework his dream grew on. Keep doing what you know to do. Keep working with excellence and inspiring people until your miracle happens, and when it happens, you will be ready for it because you have been working with excellence. All we can do is to continue loving our dream the best that we can; stewarding our dream the best we can steward it, and then pushing forward with excellence. You can accomplish all you want to accomplish when you do what you know to do with excellence.

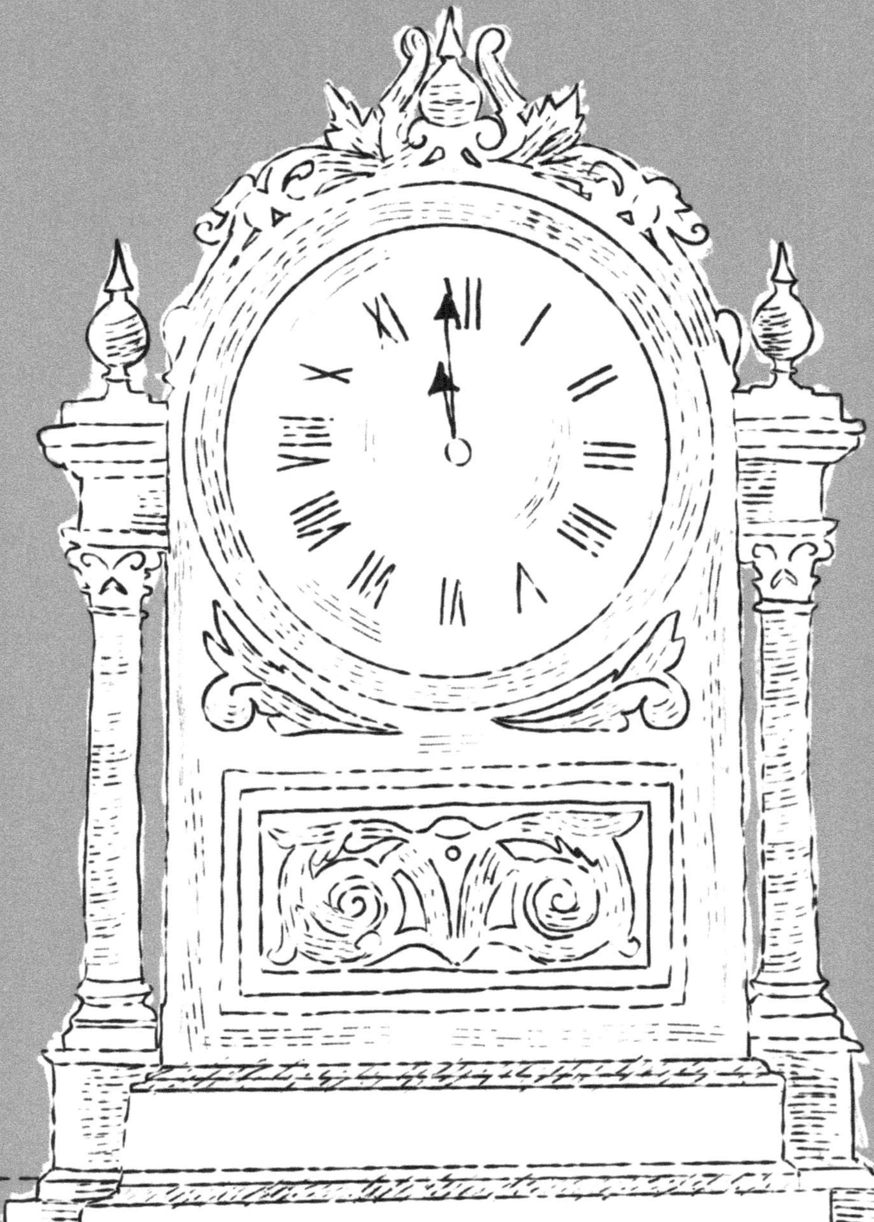

Chapter Three

MODEL WHAT YOU WANT

☐n the middle of the night, Jiminy finds his way to Geppetto's glowing fire to warm himself from the crisp mountain air. As he surveys his new hospice, away from the cold world outside, he is struck by the amount of beautiful crafts that adorn the workshop. Every available space on the wall is taken, as stockpiles overflow onto tables and benches. In the candlelight, intricate clocks tick back and forth like a midnight lullaby.

Moments later, Geppetto enters the workshop, still covered in the day's dust. With paints in hand, he is ready to put the finishing touches on his passion project. Holding up a marionette, he carefully draws its expression and surveys his work with his two cohorts, a cat and a goldfish. This scenario is all too familiar to me. In fact, I'm there right now. It is currently two minutes until midnight, and my house is finally quiet. My three kiddos are asleep upstairs, my wife is curled up soundly in the next room, and I am in my office, working on my passion project.

If you looked all around my life, you would see that all the space has been taken and then some. I am surrounded by my work. It is spilling into overflow areas and piling up in the corners. Honestly, I love it. I revel in it. Each project has its own personality and charm. In fact, I started two new projects this week simply because I couldn't bear that they were not moving forward. My best work usually happens between midnight and 3 a.m. because I use this time for my passion projects.

MOST OF THE PEOPLE IN THE **"SUCCESS COLUMN"** ARE THERE BECAUSE THEY **WORKED WHILE OTHERS SLEPT,** DEDICATED THEMSELVES TO **THE LAST TEN PERCENT,** AND, MOST IMPORTANTLY, **LOVED** WHAT THEY WERE DOING.

During normal business hours, my "real job" needs me. The pace of my life is fast and furious, but I wouldn't change a thing. I love the chaos of having 45 plates spinning at the same time. I, like Geppetto, haven't stopped creating. However, I am envious there is no sign of fatigue in Geppetto. Doesn't this guy get tired? Shouldn't he at least be dragging a little? The painstaking work of his hands surrounds him, and yet he doesn't seem deterred. He is up late working on the last 10 percent that most people would have just pushed off to the next day. Entrepreneurs take note. Most of the people in the "success column" are there because they worked while others slept, dedicated themselves to the last 10 percent, and, most importantly, loved what they were doing.

Early in my entrepreneurial journey, Andrew and I worked 18–20 hours a day. We would sleep at the office, make grilled cheese sandwiches for three meals a day, and only stopped working to butter the toast. We were singularly focused on one idea, one breakthrough, one more hour of work before we would start testing; one more customer before we made money; one more opportunity to pitch an idea. We were excellent entrepreneurs who created minimally viable examples of what we ultimately wanted to see, and the lasting legacy of those days is a definition of success that should be applied universally.

EYES ON THE FUTURE

One of my biggest problems is that I live in the future. My fifth grade teacher, Mrs. Brown, would say, "Tommy, you have your head in the clouds." She also once told my mom I should use my head for something besides a hat rack and that I'd never amount to much. Boy was she wrong. That's not a necessary part of the point I'm making, but honestly, how often do you get the chance to snap back at someone who genuinely thought you'd be a failure in life 30 years later? Well, I feel better.

In truth, I was a handful. Many teachers found out just what their limits were with me. I just always wanted to be somewhere other than where I was. It was very difficult for me to focus on school activities, not because I had ADHD or any of the other things that they diagnose kids with these days, but because I was already at the end of the book, chapter, or exercise before the rest of the kids started. It wasn't an issue of intelligence, though, because I wasn't any smarter than most of my classmates. My work was often sloppy and incomplete, and I would get "close enough" with my answers. I just wanted to be done and onto the next challenge. My head wasn't in the clouds; it was in the future. Looking back, I understand this was a crucial skill for my present success as an entrepreneur, and future thinking is a skill every entrepreneur needs to master if they are going to succeed.

All leaders and entrepreneurs must cultivate the skill of looking into the future and creating their desired outcome by operating effectively in the present. While I know the forward-looking skill set is something I have always had, I want to encourage you that it can be developed. To succeed as an entrepreneur, you will need to use your future thinking skills to create a Minimally Viable Version of your dream. Geppetto did this. He wanted a boy, so he used the resources he had like wood, paint, and strings, plus his skill as a woodcarver, to create the smallest, most affordable version of his ultimate dream—a son. Starting with this Minimally Viable Version, Geppetto minimized his risk, while positively moving toward his dream, and you can too.

To determine what steps are necessary for your dream to exist in the real world, you need to use future thinking skills. My forward-looking skill has become the hallmark of my personality and effectiveness both professionally and personally. However, like most things, they manifest themselves in great and not so great ways. For example, I love creating products that don't exist yet and leading our company, but I really have to lock in and focus when I am with people I care about. Before a moment ends, I'm out the door mentally. I even start mourning special moments before they are over. Ultimately, this robs me of the joy of the moment because I'm not present. Knowing this weakness about myself makes me more intentional about being present every day, as I interact with the people I love.

I remember a time I wasn't present, and my future thinking caused me anxiety that landed me in the emergency room. I take my role as our leader and brand creator seriously, and it is a direct extension of my personality. But if something isn't working, I can slip into emotional darkness for weeks. For example, I was recently at a trade show with a large majority of the family members of the company I founded with Andrew. It was the last trade show of its kind that we would do as a solo company because we had been acquired. All of this was exciting, and we went all out both with creativity and effort. The event was a tremendous success. Through good planning and hard work, our family pulled off the impossible to make each customer experience amazing. It was a moment I should've been so proud of—had I not mentally

> TO DETERMINE WHAT STEPS ARE NECESSARY FOR YOUR DREAM TO EXIST IN THE REAL WORLD, YOU NEED TO USE FUTURE THINKING SKILLS.

and emotionally catapulted into the future. I had the margin to revel in our success, but I couldn't.

We were well staffed, so I wasn't swamped with customers, and we prepared well for capturing leads that would turn into real dollars. The new products and features we released changed the industry for the better. While I was proud of our result and the entire team's effort to get us there, the moment the doors opened and the show started, my mind immediately went to the future. I became anxious about how different things would be the next year. I started worrying about how we could maintain our level of engagement and excitement. How would we fit in to being just a product on the shelf with other products, and how would we mesh styles with other reps and brands? It was a struggle all week to maintain my normal level of excitement and enthusiasm. As a result, I experienced legitimate angst about the future that manifested in physical symptoms and landed me in the emergency room.

While successful entrepreneurs need to have the skill of future thinking, they also need to be self-aware to guard against the anxiety that can sometimes come with being in the future mentally. Personal experience has taught me to balance my future thinking skill and to use it for the strength it gives when creating a Minimally Viable Version of what I want to manifest professionally. There must be a balance for everything to coexist peacefully. So while I want you to become a future thinker, I also want you to learn the value of relishing the moment and not doubting that the future is good.

DOUBT IS NOT AN OPTION

I have always lived by the idea that everything is "figure-outable." Yes, I know that isn't a word, but the idea is true. No matter what your dream is or what you want to accomplish, with enough resources and time, you can figure anything out. Success starts with believing in yourself and believing that you can succeed at your dream. As a leader, you need to believe you have everything it takes to win.

The entire job of an entrepreneur is to get enough information to solve problems and create solutions. You don't know what you don't know, and as a leader or an entrepreneur, you have to figure it out. Most people stop when they think they can't succeed anymore because their resources are depleted, or they have run out of answers. However, if you just give an idea a little more time and effort, you can and will figure it out if you believe in yourself. The minute you start to doubt is when you fail. You can overcome every challenge you are facing by believing you have the skills you need and that everything is "figure-outable."

Don't make the choice to give into fear and doubt. While doubting yourself is normal, letting it stop you is a choice. I get up every day with the choice to doubt or to believe in myself, but I don't let doubt stop me. I push past it, and so can you. Stay on mission. As leaders, we make the hard choice to move forward in the face of doubt. If you are feeling unsure about any area you want to move forward in, then the thing to do is to prepare. While I don't like the work involved in preparation, it is preparation that combats doubt. If you want to doubt less, then prepare more, and the way to prepare for success as an entrepreneur is by creating a Minimally Viable Version of your dream.

MINIMALLY VIABLE VERSION IN FOUR STEPS

When I am launching into a new area, I have four steps I take for creating a Minimally Viable Version of my dream. In the first step, I want you to imagine the finished product, your dream, built out in its entirety. For this step, you will need to grab a pencil and paper or use a whiteboard so you can write all the details you can think of. No detail is too small to be skipped. Think about all of your senses, account for them on your list, and imagine the user's experience. How do you want them to feel when they engage with your product or dream? Your dream may not encompass all five senses, but spending time crossing them off your list will guarantee you at least considered them. I like to use a whiteboard for this part of the exercise because I can stand back and look at it from afar, which gives me perspective. The act of stepping away from the work helps me visualize things at a higher level.

Once you have your list compiled of all the details, grab another sheet of paper or whiteboard, and begin to group the details together. Being able to see patterns and familiarities is a skill every leader needs in their tool belt, and this is great practice for that. But don't feel like everything needs a group. Some things are genuinely going to be outliers, but most things should have at least a few associated details attached to it. Now, you can name these groups.

The names you give these groups will help you identify the high-level concepts of your project that need to be focused on. For example, if it's your dream to have an online store for vintage clothing and you listed 10,000 followers on Instagram and the same on Facebook ,and those two details got lumped into a group, you might name that group "Social Media Presence." Now, are you going to gain 10,000 followers tomorrow? No. But did listing the details and grouping them together give you a clear picture of one of the high-level concepts you needed to identify to get started? Absolutely.

CONSIDER WHAT YOU CAN ACCOMPLISH NOW THAT WILL MOVE YOU TOWARD YOUR DREAM.

The second step is to take each concept one at a time to assess if there is an easily attainable version of the finished product you can create with your current resources. There is no reason not to have a section of your vision that is fully developed if it is easy to accomplish and doesn't handicap the rest of the project. While you're building your online vintage clothing store, if your dream is to have a fully functional website where you add pictures of sourced clothing and people make transactions, then there are many low-cost options for you to have this running in minutes and customized in days. Strategically, attack the things that can be done now with the resources you have now. But this isn't permission to only do the enjoyable things. This is an exercise in the elimination of goals. I like to break my high-level groups into two camps: achievable now and achievable later.

The third step is to take the "achievable later" group and determine if, as a high-level group, there is a smaller version of that set of goals that can be achieved now. You may have a high-level group called "Quality Vintage Inventory" that details: 4,500 pieces of inventory online, focused on 1940–1965, 70 percent of women's clothing, natural and synthetic fibers. You can achieve the concept of Quality Vintage Inventory on a much smaller scale than 4,500 pieces. Currently, you may only be able to source clothes from the 1960s or only be able to run 50 percent of your inventory in women's styles. Do what you can now with the resources you have now.

This doesn't mean you have to change your vision for the end goal, but the end goal doesn't mean you should wait to start your dream until that's what you can achieve out of the gate. It is a win when I can make any progress in any of my detailed areas. Consider what you can accomplish now that will move you toward your dream. In this step, I change the details to match my capabilities at the moment and copy them into the "achievable now" category. Doing this keeps me from stopping any emotional momentum I have simply because my abilities don't currently match up to my dream. Emotional momentum at this stage is crucial because every win will ride on sheer determination and effort. These early days are critical to your success and keeping your head above water right now is just a matter of attitude. The easiest way to kill the dream in the early days is to compare what you have with what you want.

The fourth step is to decide out of the lot that is left what is actually "mission critical." Not every detail is going to be necessary for the beginning of your Minimally Viable Version. You may have an entire grouping named "Team Members." This grouping will likely include details like 10–15 customer service people, COO and CFO, three web designers, design consultants, and product managers. At the earliest stage, you may not be able to hire any of these people, but don't worry because they are not critical to your start, even though they may be critical to your finish. You will find the right time along the way to add them to the team by using this exercise again and again as you grow.

MY MINIMALLY
VIABLE VERSION

Recently, I partnered with some local restaurateurs to buy a popular music venue in our downtown corridor about a block away from our offices. It had a great reputation in our local music scene, but over the last few years, as the music touring scene has declined, the venue struggled. The building needed some refreshing and the concept of the bar needed to be reworked. For several months, we slowly changed the menu and the venue while continuing its tradition of live music. Next, we had to make the tough decision of what we wanted the future of the business to be. Did we want to hang on to the tried-and-true concept that was just getting by, or did we want to take a risk, throw it all to the wind, and try something new and exciting? One guess at what we did—we did the new and exciting thing, because that's who I am.

I wanted to do an outdoor bar and community space on a large scale in our downtown area for some time. On half an acre with green space, fire pits, and water features, I envisioned a bar that was a combination: arcade; beer garden; tailgate; concert venue; and backyard cookout. The problem was that I didn't have the million dollars it would take to create such a space downtown. In the past, the inability to create the full-blown future I imagined would have paralyzed me. But now, as an experienced entrepreneur, I create a Minimally Viable Version for what I want in the future. I inventoried the resources I had, which included a 5,000 square foot music venue that was struggling as a business and a cavernous music hall that was begging for new life. With a little imagination, I scaled down the concept from half an acre, roughly 22,000 square feet, to fit inside the available space to create a brand new concept.

I would never have approached this project like this as a rookie entrepreneur. As a novice entrepreneur, I would have set off to find investors for my crazy dream, and I would have tried to convince someone to give me the million dollars so I could complete my plan of creating this ultra-cool bar. Or maybe I would have done a roadshow. Armed with an executive summary of my dream and a slick slide deck, I would traverse meeting after meeting, pitch after pitch, explaining the benefits of community space and how the new concept allowed us to be unique in our market and to operate on much smaller margins. In the end, I would wind up road worn, depressed, out of words, and leaking passion with no way to refill the tank.

Believe me, nothing destroys passion about a dream like other people constantly saying they don't share your enthusiasm, or worse, feeling the need to tell you all the reasons it won't work instead of just telling you no. How do I know? Because that's how our first company went. Although I learned a lot of lessons that you can only really know by making mistakes firsthand, the business ended up going nowhere. In the past, I spent so much time trying to convince others they should invest in us, in our whole grandiose idea of becoming a national brand, that I failed at being an effective local brand. Sometimes you need to scale back the vision and bring clarity on a small scale—the Minimally Viable Version—for the dream to move forward.

I wonder if Geppetto ever struggled with this. He was creative, like me. He was a business owner, like me. His life depended on his ability to be ahead of the market and build products based on expectations of future needs, like me. Okay, maybe that last one is a stretch, but I still like to imagine Geppetto hovered over a workbench, looking at plans to make the coolest music box the world had ever seen. I can see him spending hours pacing around his cramped little shop, looking at all the work hanging around him while talking aloud to his cat, Figaro, about how his new idea was going to revolutionize bedtime for hundreds of little children.

I wonder if he ever got together a group of Angel Investors from the village and pitched them his new design, only for them to tell him all the things wrong with his "product-market fit." I can hear them telling Geppetto how much they love his concept and how they might consider investing if he would just change 80 to 90 percent of his idea to fit one they already have ownership in. Fellow entrepreneurs, it is a bitter, unwelcoming world out there in startup land. As much as I'd like to think that Geppetto shared my struggles, life was probably much simpler back then. He was not trying to balance cap tables and equity splits over seed rounds and figure out if he should do a convertible debt note or take on venture capital. He just kept carving. But that doesn't mean he wasn't making strides toward his dreams.

Geppetto was doing what I had to learn to do the hard way. He created a small version of his dream with what he could do instead of trying to create the end product with none of the resources. He could see in his heart his hoped-for son. He imagined his son's clothes and his hair color. Geppetto even imagined Pinocchio's expression and took extra care to get it just right. When he finished painting Pinocchio, he danced him around the workshop and mimicked what would be Pinocchio's trademark mischievous personality. Geppetto had no shortage of vision.

THE SYSTEM

Geppetto's work was not representative of the scope of his dream, just the scope of his resources. You can break every dream down into a smaller version of itself (the Minimally Viable Version) that can be accomplished at your current level of resources. Today, as the potential for a new and exciting challenge came to the forefront of my attention, I dashed into the future to see what it looked like and immediately started reverse engineering everything back to the place in time I currently stood.

GEPPETTO'S WORK WAS NOT REPRESENTATIVE OF THE SCOPE OF HIS DREAM, JUST THE SCOPE OF HIS RESOURCES.

Typically, if I can do that, I get pretty enthused about the idea, whatever it is, because it means I can make it happen with a little hard work and usually a few lucky breaks.

The only thing you need to do as an entrepreneur to win is to just keep going. The only difference between the people who succeed and the people who don't is that the people who don't make it—stopped. Winning is only a matter of will. If you haven't made it to your dream, but you are still going, then there is still a chance. Change the game, change the rules, get the skills, and achieve your dream! All you have is now. What are you doing with it?

When outside forces brought their abilities to bear on Geppetto's behalf, it was the smaller version of his dream that they utilized to expand and animate Pinocchio. What if Geppetto had never done what he could? Would he have squandered the opportunity of a lifetime because he had not prepared during the lifetime of the opportunity? Would he have been asked to create a wooden boy to house the miracle? Would that have caused him to rush and cut corners so he could possess his miracle faster? We will never know what would have been because when it was time to have a miracle performed, Geppetto was ready. Today, execute toward your dream for tomorrow so you can be ready too.

Geppetto took his vision and accomplished what he could. He scaled his plans to achieve a smaller version of his dream using what he had. He could easily source clothes. He decided on a disposition and painted on an expression. He even provided his stand-in son a name, Pinocchio. The most important lesson you have to learn about building your dreams is that there are no shortcuts to "fully alive" dreams. Set clear goals in activating the "Minimally Viable Version" of your passion project and move toward your future.

Chapter Four

GETTING THE WIN THROUGH PARTNERSHIPS

My entrepreneurial desires started years before my dream of running my business became a reality. Years passed before I saw even a hint of opportunity. I don't think Geppetto birthed his desire to have a son overnight, either. Like my dream, his desire to be a father was probably a long felt, unrelenting, deep-seated hope that sometimes felt like it would never happen. I can relate.

Like Geppetto, I always had the spark of the entrepreneur in me. As a child, I was always one to make the rules rather than follow them, and I would rather game the system than play by it. Eventually, gaming the system wasn't something I did out of necessity; it was something I did out of nature. I rarely followed "the plan" when it came to my education. Early on, I would see how far ahead of my classmates I could get. Weeks into the semester,

I would have completed the entire year's worth of class and homework assignments, but, after all of that extra effort, I wouldn't try to advance to the next level. Instead, I would coast through the rest of my time being what many teachers called a "general distraction to others."

I was able to lobby the school district to create a class called Independent Science Investigations as a pilot when I needed one more science credit on my high school transcript to graduate, but I didn't want to take advanced biology. This class allowed me and five other co-conspirators to independently and without actual curriculum, develop a semester-long science experiment, carry it out, and present the results for credit. We were done in a matter of weeks, not months, and my graduation was secured.

My first day on my college campus for freshman orientation, I learned that our school didn't actually have a mascot. So I sought out the head of men's athletics and volunteered for the job. I designed the costume, procured the parts and pieces, and secured a half ride scholarship for just volunteering to be a costumed idiot a couple hours a week. A prerequisite of knowledge, talent, or ability never stood in my way when it came to doing something I wanted. And like all entrepreneurs, I carry a supreme confidence in my aptitude for figuring things out.

MY DREAM

In my early career, I was a perpetual "number two" on the organization chart. There were things about my skill set that got me promoted to the highest levels of leadership; but there were also things about my personality (mostly the immaturity of being in my 20's) that kept me outside of consideration for being the number one. I interpreted my lack of progress to the highest level as an indictment of my abilities when in reality it was more a commentary on my capacity. I was only big enough to contain my dream.

I had not developed enough of the necessary bandwidth intellectually and emotionally to manage building the dreams of others. As a result, I always looked for opportunities to fulfill my dreams instead of serving the dreams of the leader I was under. The "my dream first" attitude stunted my growth personally and professionally. In every organization and at every important juncture, there is an opportunity to make a choice: "Do I serve me, or do I serve the mission?" In those days, I poorly chose because I didn't understand the value of partnering with others.

THEN IT HAPPENED

Andrew and I were about a year and a half into having our first startup, which means we were a year and a half without a paycheck. I had used up all of our savings, my severance from my last job was long gone, and I had a wife and a one-year-old to care for. To say things were rough would be an understatement. We were working 15 to 20 hours a day, and I was perpetually in a state of exhaustion or guilt if I was resting. The first year of my son's life is a blur that I watched mostly on videos sent to me from my wife while I was at the office. Looking back, I only kept going because if I quit, then maybe everything I thought to be true about myself and about not being capable of having my dream would prove true.

Kelly, my amazing wife, had taken a part-time job at a tanning salon so she could cover our bills. On her way to work, she called me at my office and said, "We don't have any food." My mind couldn't process what she said. "Tommy? Did you hear me?" — silence. "Tommy, we don't have any food in the house, and I'm going to need something for the baby later. I need you to come home and figure it out."

"Okay, babe," was all I could say. Without saying much to Andrew, I left the office and went home. It was worse than I expected. I had paid little attention to the stock in our pantry because Kelly always managed to put something on a plate when I was home. I started opening cabinets in our tiny kitchen to find just what she had said. No food. Nothing. Every cabinet empty. The fridge was the same and so was the freezer. What had I done? Where had I led us? It broke me.

What followed was the type of uncontrollable loss of control that only comes in these situations. I cried, then I sobbed. Weeping, I cursed at the empty cabinets, but really I was cursing at myself. I had stolen from my sweet family, traded their livelihood for my ambition. I was a miserable wretch of a man, and I knew it. I felt it in my bones. I have never felt more lonely, forsaken, and angry in my life, and there was nothing I could do about it.

Then it happened. My doorbell rang. When I got to the door, a pleasant face met me. I can only imagine what the terrible-looking creature staring back at her looked like. "Hi," she said with a smile. "This may sound strange, but something told me to bring you some groceries." Stunned, I watched as she unloaded a trunk full of groceries from her car.

No one on this planet knew what my family was going through at that moment and somehow, she did. She didn't judge me. She just unloaded bag after bag of groceries from her car to my front door. I wanted to say, "No," but I couldn't. Every bag, every item, chipped away at the "my dream first" attitude. I could do nothing to keep following my dream. I was at the end of my rope, and at the last possible second, someone else, not even connected to my dream, threw me a lifeline. I was never the same.

PARTNERSHIP AT ITS BEST MEANS **HAVING AN OPEN HEART AND MIND** THAT ALLOWS OTHERS TO JOIN IN YOUR MOMENTS AND TO BRING THEIR SKILLS AND PASSIONS TO BEAR ON YOUR BEHALF.

For weeks, I tried to intellectually work out the small miracle I had just witnessed. In the end, I just stopped trying. My gratitude far outweighed my curiosity. A week later, we got our first paycheck of $500, and it was for the entire month. I took my family to P.F. Chang's to celebrate. We have never been without groceries since.

I have never again been a "my dream first" person. In the weeks that followed, I realized that dreams, big or small, are never achieved in a vacuum. Success takes a person being able to lay aside their ambitions and make a way for others and the vision of the organization. Now, I am constantly looking for the moments when I can step into a situation and cause massive impact because I want to be that person standing on someone's doorstep offering a lifeline.

My life is dotted with the "then it happened," whatever "it" ends up being. The trick is to see the opportunity and join in during the moments when your involvement will bring the greatest impact. Partnership at its best means having an open heart and mind that allows others to join in your moments and to bring their skills and passions to bear on your behalf. If you can accomplish your dream on your own, then your dream isn't big enough. Geppetto needed partnerships, and he was aided by those around him. Geppetto's team served the mission instead of serving themselves.

GETTING THE WIN

Here is something you should know about me—I just want to win. Nothing else matters to me except the win, and because of that, I am passionate about partnering with others. Geppetto would never have experienced his miracle if it wasn't for others. Geppetto needed Figaro to open the window to let the blue fairy in. He needed the blue fairy to turn Pinocchio into a miracle, and he needed Jiminy to help guide Pinocchio once he came to life. For Geppetto, there would never have been a win without partnerships. The secret to the win is finding magic through collaboration.

I'm always looking for ways to go faster, better, and smoother, and never does this happen alone. There is an old African proverb that says, "If you want to go fast, go alone, but if you want to go far, go together." But I disagree with this saying, because I think either one requires togetherness. If you find someone who runs faster than you, then even if you go together, you will still go faster than you would have alone. So find someone who runs faster than you and you will go faster and further than you can imagine because partnership is where the magic happens.

By nature, I have always been a collaborator because I have always wanted things bigger than I could do by myself. Partnership is a function of being a hard-core achiever and needing the win. In fact, I'm so hard-core about achieving that I don't celebrate wins, because once my team and I have won, I'm ready to move on to the next opportunity to win. This drive to achieve and win is a defining characteristic of an entrepreneur, and getting the win happens through collaboration. I can win more, win better, and win bigger if I am not by myself.

I have never been the most talented guy at anything, so I always look for ways to saddle my horse with people who are the best at their area of expertise in a place I want to win. As a result, I have gone farther and faster than I ever could have on my own. This is what Jiminy Cricket did. In the opening scene of Pinocchio, Jiminy Cricket makes his appearance, and he is a complete hobo. However, because Jiminy saddled his horse to Geppetto's dream, he was able to facilitate part of Pinocchio's miracle and get some great swag in the process.

Partnering with Geppetto in this way fundamentally changed who Jiminy was. Through this collaboration, Jiminy got new clothes and an upgrade. But it didn't stop there. Everyone in this story went further and faster because of partnership and teamwork. Without this partnership, Jiminy would have remained a destitute hobo, looking for the next warm house and the next warm meal. Collaboration changed Jiminy just as much as Jiminy changed the partnership. And Jiminy didn't care who got the credit, and I relate. I couldn't care less who gets the credit, as long as there is a win.

OPTIMIZATION

There aren't any negatives to partnerships because the win is about optimization. Any extra effort beyond what you can give is better for you. There aren't any negatives to partnerships; there is only net gain. However, partnerships and relationships require effort, and you can only give emotional effort one place at a time because no one can multitask. Emotional multitasking is impossible. If you must give a lot of energy into the relationship of your partner, then you cannot give the same amount of emotional energy to your business.

Optimization is about finding someone who requires little emotional energy or someone who gets emotional energy from the same place as you. For example, if they are the "winner-type" then you will both draw emotional energy from the same place and be focused on the same goal—the win. How you and your partner approach the win may be different, but optimization happens if you both draw emotional energy from the same place. My partner, Andrew, is the grinder leader type who is always going to outwork everyone, but mostly he wants to win. Fairness is Andrew's principle driver. He believes it isn't fair if he works hard and doesn't win. As a result, Andrew outworks everyone because it is the way he guarantees the win that he deserves.

GAP COVER

I don't care if I deserve to win or not because I just want to win. If that means I have to push, pull, and finagle, then I will. Andrew's hard work and my vision always work for us and optimize our win. When we partner, then there is always a way

TO WIN, YOU NEED TO INTENTIONALLY BRING YOUR BEST SELF TO EVERY SITUATION.

to go further, faster. It's magic. And that is what collaboration does—it makes the miraculous happen further and faster. When you partner with others, it optimizes your potential and helps you get the win. Through collaboration, the possibilities are limitless.

To win, you need to intentionally bring your best self to every situation. But what about when you can't bring your best self? What happens when you have a deficit? Being less than yourself is dangerous, because when you are less than yourself and you are by yourself, then you are in total lack and you won't get the win. But if you are less than yourself and you are with someone else, then the other person picks up the slack and fills the gap. Even better, when you are less than yourself and you are with a team, then everyone gets to make up the difference—further, faster. Collaboration and partnership is what I call gap cover.

POTENTIAL

Partnerships don't diminish the win; partnerships maximize the potential to win. When choosing a partner, you want to look for potential over skill. You can teach skill, but you can't teach potential. Finding the right people really comes down to a few basic filters I apply at the top end of the decision process:

» Are they "vision first" people?

» Can they bring impact to the situation?

» Are they going to cause Then it happened moments?

» Has my familiarity clouded my view of my available resources?

» Am I overlooking someone?

» What do I need to plant most in this season? (Notice I didn't say what do I need most? If you are asking that question it is too late to plant; you have to purchase.)

» Is someone that has departed my organization or outside of my organization necessary for the vision to happen?

» Do they require extra grace?

In determining potential, I analyze what I call the "soil" of someone by asking questions like: What are the last five books that you read? How busy is your life? Do you have a lot of distractions?

I also want to know how stable their family life is. While I can't directly ask this question, I can get an idea by asking the person to tell me about themselves. I say something like, "As much as you are comfortable, tell me about yourself." Being a good interviewer is helpful and, as you find commonality, you can discover what type of soil they have. Picking your team in this way is what I call the purchasing potential for growing a harvest later, and you have a higher potential to optimize your results. Harvesting someone's potential is incredible and only happens in partnership.

The principle you use in finding a spouse is to spend enough time with them where you know who they are in every season. You know what their character is when they are sick, tired, anxious, or when they are well, happy, and celebratory. Situations can bring surprises, but you don't want surprises about their character. This same principle applies to finding a business partner. Most likely you won't have the luxury of time to see them in every season, but you can vet them in every season. In the hiring process, everyone is only going to give you glowing references of praise. Knowing this, ask for the actual fruit that you want for your next season. Ask potential partners for references from seasons that matter to you. If you know their character, then you will know the fruit that will ultimately come.

When picking your team, you might say to them, "I want two references from a time when you were stressed and felt overworked. I need a reference for when you were discouraged. How did you respond?" However, you have to ask about both seasons, so you will also need to ask, "How do you like to celebrate, and what makes you laugh?" Being able to laugh and celebrate together with your partner is important. This might be uncomfortable in the hiring process, but it will be worth it in the long run and will serve you best in picking your team and getting you the win.

Remember, you are picking a partner, not a project. When you

THE DESIRE TO **HONOR AND CELEBRATE** OTHERS IS CRUCIAL TO ANY LEADER'S VIEW OF THEIR TEAM.

go shopping for vegetables, you look for what you want based on the recipe you are making. You sort through all the vegetables to make sure you purchase the right ones; you never blindly purchase anything. This is what the hiring process is and what picking your team looks like. In the future, where do I want to be and what fruit will I want to have?

SEASONALITY

Every dream, every action, every consequence, every person, everything has a life cycle. Identifying the life cycle for things is one of those weird skills I possess. I developed it early in life. As an unpopular kid in middle school, friendships were the first thing I realized were seasonal. Kids can be brutal, and no one is more fickle than seventh and eighth graders. It's a demonic cocktail of hormones and transitional awkwardness, and I was a late bloomer.

I was bullied, but we didn't call it that. Kids just being kids, is what I heard more than one teacher say. Well, I know some kids that should have been hired as mercenaries. One kid, in particular, was on another level, though. One moment we would be friends, and then the wind would change, and he would decide he needed to pummel me. I never knew what was happening from moment to moment with him. I know some of you may read this and think, "Just avoid the guy … it's one guy, how hard could that be?" Well, I was one student in a class of 18 in a middle school of 55, so it was pretty hard.

Other kids took his lead, and for a few years there, things were touch and go with me socially. As a middle schooler, I had to develop skills that most adults don't possess. I learned quickly to sniff out a setup. I can read a room and whether it's hostile instantly. My negotiating skills are off the chart because I had to talk myself out of black eye situations on a daily basis. But most importantly, I realized that nothing, and I mean nothing, even bullying, lasts forever. If you can realize that life is seasonal, then success can become something you farm instead of something you hope for, and it always starts with—your people.

Attuning to the seasonality of your team's skills helps to know when to plant them for maximum return. I always try to remember that today's planting is tomorrow's resource. If you refuse to understand that you should plant in the planting season, regardless of need, you will be perpetually short on resources when the seasons change, because the growth that needed to happen with your team to supply the necessary answers and other resources never happened. Seasonality as a mindset is crucial to having the right people at the right time.

Understanding that everything is seasonal fixes your perspective. If you have the worst day ever or you are in a tough season, you can tell yourself, *this too will pass*. The idea of *this too will pass* gives you grace for each moment, for others, and for yourself. If you are in a moment where you failed, then you can remind yourself *this too will pass*, because failure doesn't last. Seasonality helps you understand that if you fail in a moment, you can take a deep breath and realize that you just got a new moment. It may not be a new moment where the failure isn't stinging or the consequences aren't still here, but you can realize with each new breath is a new moment to move forward.

Seasonality gives you patience because the idea of seasons means waiting. Everything in life is seed, time, and harvest. Seasonality helps you to engage your future thinking in the way where, if you want something in the next season, you will intentionally plant it now. Today's planting is tomorrow's resource. If you find yourself in a season where you are missing something, then you failed to plant it in the previous season.

BATTLING THE FAMILIAR

I have always thought Pinocchio should have been titled, "Oh Wow, a Talking Cricket!" After all, it is the first supernatural thing that we encounter in the story. It isn't named that though. In fact, we gloss right over it. Why is that? My guess is familiarity. We get introduced to the voice of the miracle moments before we see Jiminy. Familiarity builds quickly though, and because of that there is a level of sameness we build that takes some of the edge off the mental hurdle that a talking cricket is going to be handling our introduction to the story. It works great as a way to introduce a narrator; not so good for leaders.

The scariest and the trickiest part of leading for me is battling familiarity. It is the enemy of honor and celebration. The desire to honor and celebrate others is crucial to any leader's view of their team. When you look to honor and celebrate, your focus has to be on the strengths and positive traits of those around you. Focusing on your team member's strengths will help you have a better chance of plugging the right people into the right moments where they can create maximum impact. By communicating to them their strengths and why you chose them for a particular assignment, you set the expectation that they will focus on that strength. This approach encourages them to give maximum effort and focus in the area you chose them to participate. Also, this approach maximizes their buy-in, their effectiveness, and their results.

Familiarity, even just for a moment, makes us forget the incredible gift our teammates are. When familiarity sets in, we abuse people and treat them like they are replaceable. In organizations where familiarity is prevalent, there is high turnover and burnout. The vision doesn't outweigh the effort, and the team feels undervalued. In these organizations, there is always a "my dream first" leader at the helm.

Every person on your team is borrowed. They are all there for a purpose, but they are all not fully deployed all the time. Some skill sets are only going to be needed in crisis situations, for example, or when a customer needs to be saved and you need to pour some honey on a wound. We all have that one person we trust to get to the bottom of a problem and save the account or client relationship when it all hits the fan.

Jiminy Cricket, the blue fairy, Figaro, and even Cleo (the goldfish), all had specific support roles for Geppetto's dream to become a reality, and Geppetto needed them. They each played a part in preparing him for his dream, walking with him through the lean times where the dream felt out of reach. Geppetto's partners facilitated his dream through their actions and watched over and managed the dream to success. Like these characters, your teammates will all have different capacities for action, they will all have a different bearing on the result, and they will all have different seasonal effectiveness.

PLENTY ENOUGH

It may feel fun to think of entrepreneurship as a cutthroat game of competition, but that isn't the reality. There is an unlimited supply of purpose. When you find yourself imagining the competition, then you are in a place where your work (the purpose of your win) doesn't matter. The idea that there is only one way to win, or one winner, is false, and this mindset will keep you from partnering with others. Others don't have to lose for you to win.

There is more than enough success to go around. When you succeed, you aren't taking it out of someone else's hands. You aren't taking food off someone else's plate. Sometimes you may work on the same deal as someone else, but that isn't what I'm talking about. There is no lack when it comes to success. There are plenty of fish out there. Sometimes you might compete over the same fish, but that doesn't mean you are going to run out of fish.

Geppetto and Jiminy understood this. They didn't contend with each other, and they weren't in competition with anyone else. Geppetto wasn't running around trying to trick other woodcarvers and looking for ways to commit arson on local clock shops. Instead, he realized his dream by partnering with others. He went further, faster, and experienced a miracle. Through collaboration, you will too!

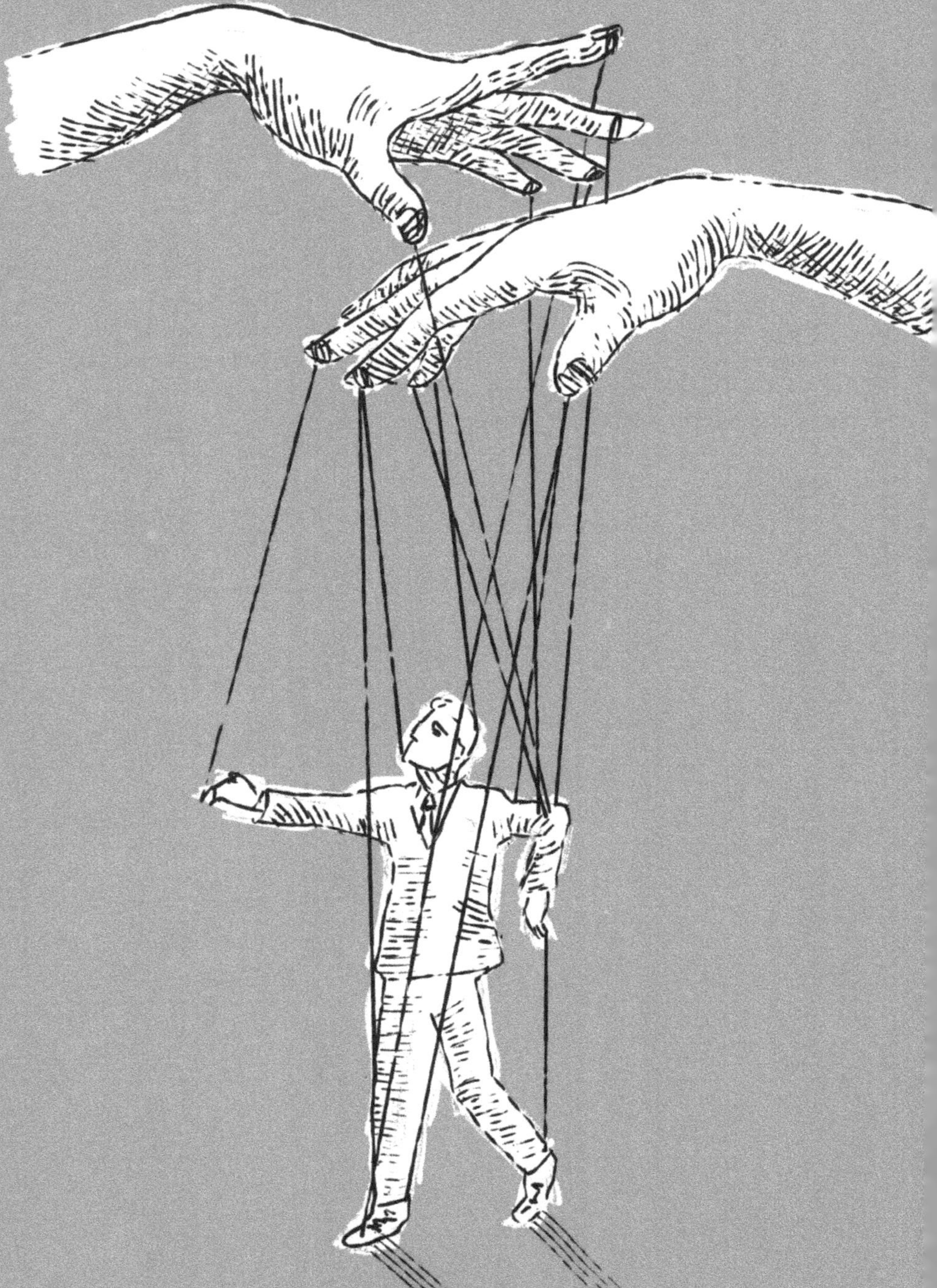

Chapter Five

NAVIGATING THE MIRACULOUS

How many times have you agonized over the feeling that somehow you just didn't fit in? Whether with a colleague, your team, or even your corporation, one of these things is not like the other. More times than I would like to admit that "one thing" was always—me. These were the early days of my entrepreneur journey when I didn't realize being different was magic. Instead of embracing what made me unique, I was like Pinocchio just trying to fit in. When I looked at the puppets around me and realized I had no strings, rather than celebrating this, I looked for approval from others, and ultimately tried to glue strings onto myself—never a good idea. We are uniquely made, but tragically, most of us just want to fit in.

My moment of realization came as a bit of a surprise. I spent most of my life feeling weird and out of place—marginalized, but I was facing a season where instinctively I knew I needed permission to be myself. The business I built had just sold, and I had stayed on as an employee to help with the transition. I was struggling to fit in with the new corporate structure. I went from being the dad of a family to being an employee of a corporation.

I always ran my business like a family. I wasn't the CEO; I was the dad. Instead of making people feel like they worked for me, I created an atmosphere where people felt like they worked with me. All of our meetings were family meetings, and our uniqueness was celebrated. However, now I found myself in a situation where I didn't fit into the corporate setting and some people around me seemed like they were going out of their way not to like me. Ouch!

One night, it hit me, and I thought, I'm not going to pull a Pinocchio. Pinocchio was one-of-one, a supernatural phenomenon, but he missed his miracle because all he wanted to do was fit in. This is what happens when we marginalize ourselves and others. It always ends in tragedy. Every successful leader and entrepreneur needs to get one thing right; the things that make you unique and different are the very things that bring the magic. I'm passionate about helping you unlock the miraculous inside of you. But for this to happen, you have to make marginalization illegal personally and within your team.

The word marginalized means to treat something or someone with insignificance or to render them powerless. When we marginalize what makes us different or a miracle, then we render powerless the very thing we need to win. In order for you to win, all of who you are needs to show up fully. But this won't happen if you have decided your miracle, how you are wired, and what you are gifted to do isn't of value. Pinocchio was one-of-one in the entire universe. There was no one like him, yet he desperately wanted to be common so he could fit in. He wanted to be one of a million, a real boy, instead of being the miracle he was. As tragic as this is, we all pull a Pinocchio. We are uniquely made with creative talents and abilities; however, what most of us want is to just fit in.

One of my favorite scenes from the Pinocchio movie is the sequence when he is forced on stage by the puppeteer Stromboli. It's important because it's in this scene he realizes he's different. Realizing places of difference is the first step to discovering the miraculous. One of the quirky things about the miraculous is that they are often rooted in the things that make us different, not the things that make us the same. However, our miracle will often facilitate unity and not division. When we see our differences as strengths, we build a more powerful unit instead of making a homogenous mess of sameness.

Until this point in the story, Pinocchio had only focused on what he wasn't. He was not a real boy. All he could see was his deficient state of existence, and he focused on his personal differences as if they were something he lacked, instead of something that made him stand out. This led him into the arms of "Honest John," the character that would traffic him into service to Stromboli. Just like Pinocchio, when you focus on your differences as if they are deficiencies, you open up the door to be taken advantage of by people who see your value and want it for themselves.

OUR MIRACLE WILL OFTEN FACILITATE UNITY AND NOT DIVISION.

Although Pinocchio was now a slave to a puppet master, something marvelous happened in Pinocchio's life. It was here, in the traveling sideshow, when he was placed next to other wooden puppets, that he first realized he wasn't one of them either. What a strange moment this must have been for him. In Pinocchio's most desperate moment, we find him having a large personal breakthrough. He comes face-to-face with being in the transitional phase of life between who he was and who he is becoming.

Like Pinocchio, this moment of realization that his differences set him apart is necessary for every person who hopes to become a miracle. I can't begin to empathize with what he was feeling. His entire paradigm of understanding was being rewritten in front of a live audience. It's like finding out on national television that you're adopted and that your father is Superman, and he's been waiting to tell you you're special and have all these powers, and that you're not really from Earth and can leap buildings and stop bullets. The amount of information that had to be processed at that moment must have been staggering.

Pinocchio was also interacting with lifeless versions of himself, which, let's admit, is just weird. Then he is forced into a live performance with his conscious scowling at him from the corner. He doesn't know the steps, and he has to make up the routine on the fly. Ultimately, there is no promise of any type of reward for all this effort. There are parts of this I can relate to, but surely no one has had a more public meltdown of all they know to be true than poor Pinocchio.

I have experienced those awkward moments in front of peers and colleagues where it was evident to me I was different. I have always worked with incredibly talented people, but I always, in one way or another, just didn't fit in. I understand the desire to feel connected and be accepted, and it will seem in those moments that the quickest pathway to harmony is marginalizing yourself, but don't do it. I have realized that other members of the team are "lifeless," and I have had to realize that sometimes being fully alive and understanding your miraculous nature reveals the limitations of the other players on stage. That is never a fun or welcome moment in my experience. It's weird and uncomfortable for everyone. What I often fail to remember in those moments is that we are all on different journeys with a different miracle. And as beautiful as miracles are, they always cause a degree of friction.

My desire to be recognized as a miracle is matched only by Pinocchio's desire to be a real boy. I am far too often caught up in making sure others validate my miracle with external praise or acceptance, and that's when everything hits the fan. That desire to be validated is insecurity winning the race to control my thoughts instead of a desire to serve the mission. To help me navigate the miraculous to better serve the vision I have developed five simple rules:

- Rule #1: There are no rules for miracles.

- Rule #2: Miracles always appear to serve someone else.

- Rule #3: Don't get caught up in the strings of others.

- Rule #4: When miracles don't get valued, they get abused.

- Rule #5: When in doubt, refer to rule #1.

RULE #1: THERE ARE NO RULES FOR MIRACLES.

If Pinocchio let the rules dictate his actions, then he would never have discovered his miraculous ability. What would have happened if Pinocchio looked around at all the other marionettes and said, "They have strings. I should have strings! I'm not moving another inch until I get strings!" This seems ridiculous to us because we know the story, but this is what we do when we marginalize ourselves by trying to change so we will fit into the crowd. But a miracle is just that—it's a miracle. It's something outside of time, space, and expectation. Miracles transcend all rules to serve those around you.

We have a saying in my company, and it has become our rallying cry, "Rule number one is, the rules don't apply." The rules never apply for a miracle. That should be true in all cases simply because of the definition of the word "miracle." However, it is much easier for us to accept the abstract thought we are "miracles" at a surface level than to embrace the staggering implications and responsibilities of being a miracle in our hearts, and subsequently our daily lives and behaviors. When a rule, whether it be written, societal, or strategic, challenges the nature of the miracle or vision, you should always challenge the rule, not the vision. The vision in your heart and mind does not exist to serve the rules because the rules exist to serve the vision. Rules provide guidance and establish hard fought boundaries that are often the result of lessons learned through failure and trials, so they should not be taken lightly, but rules should always be treated as a tool to protect the vision and to protect the miracle. Rules should never be treated as the vision.

RULE #2: MIRACLES ALWAYS APPEAR TO SERVE SOMEONE ELSE.

One of the most beautiful things about the miraculous is that it is never self-serving. Is there a level of notoriety that comes with the territory? Sure. But I have never seen the miraculous used effectively for the promotion of self. There is always a benefactor for the miraculous that is not the miracle. I learned this the hard way.

AS A STEWARD OF YOUR MIRACLE, YOU CARRY THE RESPONSIBILITY IMPLIED BY YOUR NATURE AS A MIRACLE.

When I started my first business, I had complete confidence I would succeed. It felt like this was the moment I had been waiting for my whole life where I could completely be myself. I was ready to go full force and full volume. I wanted to prove to everyone that fully loaded Tommy (the things that made me miraculous) was how it should be; however, I failed to see that my miracle was never meant to be self-serving. As a result, this business failed miserably. Mistakenly, I thought my miracle was to validate me, but miracles never get used for self-validation.

Being unique and one-of-one in the universe, qualifies you to be a miracle. My miracle is that I am incredibly gifted at taking very complicated facts and information and simplifying them so everyone understands. If you give me enough time and data, I will figure it out, no matter the problem. But the moment I realized my miracle existed for others, everything changed. When I help others to become the best they can be, I win. This is what it looks like when our miracle serves others. Think about boats sitting in a harbor. If I raise the tide, every boat will rise. When I co-elevate or, in other words, when I use my miracle to help someone else, everyone benefits. If I have a my-boat-only mentality, I marginalize my miracle, and not only do I lose, but everyone around me loses. Miracles never exist for themselves.

If you are uniquely positioned, gifted, or talented, and you have accepted the fact that you are a miracle, then the first bridge you have to cross is that you don't exist for yourself, because miracles are never self-serving. I use this as the litmus test in my own life. Often, I consider if I am trying to use my miracle to help others or promote myself. When I spot the selfishness in it, I try to eradicate it. It is a matter of self-preservation, or you could say, miracle-preservation.

I want it to be a miracle, and to see my life impact others in a radical way that forever changes the trajectory of their hopes and dreams, while encouraging and inspiring them. I want their lives to be better because I have meaningful relationships with them, and I bring my strengths and abilities to fight on their behalf. Miracles are not yours, and they always appear to serve someone else. As a steward of your miracle, you carry the responsibility implied by your nature as a miracle.

RULE #3: DON'T GET CAUGHT UP IN THE STRINGS IF YOU AREN'T SUPPOSED TO HAVE ANY.

One of the funniest moments in the "Got no strings on me," song is when Pinocchio gets tangled up in the other puppets. Here he is, singing his freedom song, when he gets into a knotted mess. He got too close and didn't see the danger. The snare was set. One misstep and he went from a freewheeling balladeer to endangering the entire show. What I often find true is that when we deny our miraculous nature, it is easy to get entwined with those who choose to stay tied down. When that happens, it not only limits us but often makes the situation worse. It is difficult for a person with supernatural freedom to coexist with a puppet and not mess up everything within reach. It grinds the whole production to a halt and causes chaos. My advice is to avoid this at all costs.

Believe me, strings come in all shapes and sizes. I like to define strings as: self-imposed expectations that are not relevant to the vision, contrary to the truth, or otherwise placed by outside sources and made valid by our agreement. You see how easy it would be to be entangled with this mess? Miracles require a lot. Don't add on to those requirements with additional ridiculous expectations that aren't necessary to capture the dream you have. Likewise, don't accept any expectations that others disguise as "facts" that are contrary to the soul of the vision. It's in accepting this outside input that we give it power and ultimately enable it to sidetrack us.

Pinocchio got sidetracked and caught in the strings of what I call the Assumptive Comparison Paradox. The Assumptive Comparison Paradox is the awful moment when we have self-realization that should set us free and empower us, but, instead, we assume that because we aren't yet what we hope to be, we must be this "something else." Nine times out of 10 that "something else " is the furthest terrible extreme we can imagine because we magnify our disappointment of not being what we want. Our "something else" perspective colors our perception of who we are. For me, it plays out the most consistently in my view of myself as a father.

I travel out of town a lot for work, and because of where we live (a smallish city with only a hub airport) that usually means a full day and night away anytime I leave. Did I mention I have three kids? I do: Jackson, Elliot, and Sutton. My kiddos hate when I leave. But I hate it more. I know they will have fun at home and be taken care of by their amazing mother. They understand Daddy loves them and they have adjusted to my crazy schedule, but every time I walk out the door, I am constantly fighting feelings of failure as a parent. I have in my mind the dad I want to be, but because I'm not able to give my kids all of me, I immediately feel like the worst father ever.

I'm not the best father by a long shot, but there's no logical reason for me to feel like such a complete failure as a parent. My kids are well adjusted, polite, caring, and they look out for one another. They are talented and funny and genuinely some of my favorite people to be around. Kelly, my wife, gets most of the credit for that, but I contributed to their personalities too. However, The Assumptive Comparison Paradox makes me believe that since I don't compare or match up to the perfect dad version in my head, I must be the worst dad ever.

To quote the great philosopher Ricky Bobby, "If you ain't first, you're last." That's not true, obviously, but in those moments walking down my steps, suitcase in hand, it sure feels like it. It's not a fair thing to do to yourself or your teammates. It diminishes your capacity to contribute, harms your self-confidence, and

RULES ARE SIMPLY GUARD RAILS.

stunts your growth. Comparing myself to an imaginary version of myself is the quickest road to anxiety and depression for me. The spiral usually looks like this: I'm not this perfect version of myself ⇒ I must be the worst version of myself ⇒ Who would want to be around me or work with me ⇒ It would be better if I didn't contribute ⇒ NOW I AM THE WORST VERSION OF MYSELF! I constantly have to remember that version of myself is an imaginary and impossible ideal. It can't be obtained. Remembering this gives me room for emotional freedom.

Sadly, I rarely notice the spiral until I'm in the "not contributing" phase, because until that point everything was internal. The problem is that I don't see it until it's affecting others. See how this is a bad thing? As a leader and team builder, I'm working on being more proactive with my evaluation of my special differences. That keeps the best version of myself on the horizon for me to become and forever rips off the rearview mirror that only shows regret and a missed opportunity.

RULE #4: WHEN MIRACLES DON'T GET VALUED, THEY GET ABUSED.

On my phone's lock screen for the last several months has been the phrase, "What is consistently taken for granted is eventually taken away." That is never truer than when considering the nature of the miraculous. Abuse is the natural byproduct of undervaluing the miraculous. Abuse takes many forms, and almost all of them can be seen being played out with people that struggle with accepting they are miraculous.

Neglect is the first and lowest level of abuse that I experience in my own life. There are certain activities that feed the things I consider special about me. Certain environments cause my gifts and abilities to thrive. There are certain people that challenge me, and our gifts and abilities mix really well together, creating a special kind of magic when we get together. Here's the crazy part: I am 100 percent in charge of how often I do those activities, engage with those environments, and interact with those people. Even so, I go through extremely dry seasons because I don't discipline myself to actively participate in those activities, seek out those environments, or make the necessary bandwidth in my day to include fostering stronger relationships with those people. I'm not actively trying to harm the miracle inside me, but I am not actively trying to stoke the flame of activity. As a result, I create a culture of passive neglect that ultimately leads to the death of parts of my personality and ability mix that makes me special.

Self-harm is a terrible sickness. I know from personal experience the challenge that comes with thoughts of worthlessness that cloud your reality; I know what it's like to feel like everything is moving so fast and you are stuck in slow motion; I know all too well what it means to want to have other alternatives to just existing. Accepting the miraculous isn't enough. When you care for yourself because you are a carrier of the miraculous, you start to see a clear picture of how valuable you are to those around you. Understanding the capacity for the miraculous inside of yourself is key to treating yourself with the respect and dignity you deserve, and it prevents fits of self-sabotage and isolation. Realizing your miraculous capacity forces you to search out community in an attempt to find space for your miracle.

Causing pain for others is the natural last stop on this unfortunate train. The abused can become abusers. Often, I'm jealous of people that are obviously operating in the miraculous. Jealousy, when it is fully grown, gives birth to resentment and resentment harbored over time produces a crop of actions that are aimed at reducing the miraculous. We do that to tear down others mentally and emotionally so that our inadequacies are less prevalent. It stems from the guilt that we aren't living up to our potential as miracles, but ultimately disqualifies us from participation in the miracles of others. People who understand they are miraculous rightly become protective of who they let into their lives, which protects them from the abusive nature of those who seek to be taller by making others smaller. Protecting your miracle at the macro level will allow you to filter out a lot of the drama and distraction that rob you of your miraculous nature. The only difference between a colander and a coffee filter is the size of the holes. If you can reduce the size of the holes at a higher level than you previously had, you can have a much purer experience day-to-day at a micro-level where it really matters. So protect what makes you a miracle.

RULE #5: WHEN IN DOUBT, REFER TO RULE #1.

If you are ever in doubt, just remember that the rules never applied to start with. Rules are simply guard rails. Some people may have the mentality that they can drive in any lane they want because they pay taxes, but at the end of the day there are some safety measures to help keep your car on the road. Act miraculous without rules, while remembering that your miracle is to serve someone else. Nothing can stop you when you stay out of other people's strings, and you value your miracle.

As a leader and an entrepreneur, it is up to you to create an environment where marginalization is illegal. To get the win, marginalization has to be such an outlier that when it happens, it is obvious. Certain things stick out like a sore thumb, so when you, as the leader, create an environment where marginalizing yourself and others isn't normal, then if it happens, you and everyone else will notice and put a stop to it. I live near The Augusta National, which is known for having the most lush and pristine grass in the United States. If there was a rock in the middle of the fairway, you would see it from a mile away. The expectation is that this is the best grass on the planet, so if there is a bare patch or trash, it would stand out because you have preemptively determined the perception of what should be there so when it is not there, it sticks out. As the leader, you lay the grass and create the environment where the miraculous can thrive.

In this environment, everyone has a sense that they are working with one another rather than for someone else.

Making the wrong choices as a leader will always cripple the miracle. In creating Pinocchio, Geppetto picked the choice pieces of wood, and with great care, he carved the surfaces of Pinocchio. If there had been knot holes, we would have seen them, but there weren't. Geppetto joined all the parts of his miracle Pinocchio just right, so that everything was aligned. He also sanded Pinocchio down so there were no splinters. If Geppetto hadn't taken such care, then being in a public environment would have been hard for Pinocchio. All of Geppetto's attention made it easier for his miracle to function in the real world, and as a leader, that is all you are hoping to do for your team.

View your team as a miracle, and create an environment that makes it easy for their miracle to operate in the real world. That's what Geppetto did. Your miracle is worth the effort to discover and develop, but it won't reveal itself until you are ready to let it serve others. Just like Pinocchio was a miracle, you have unique gifts and talents that are just waiting for you to explore. Raise the tide in your life, and in the process, you will raise the tide for everyone around you.

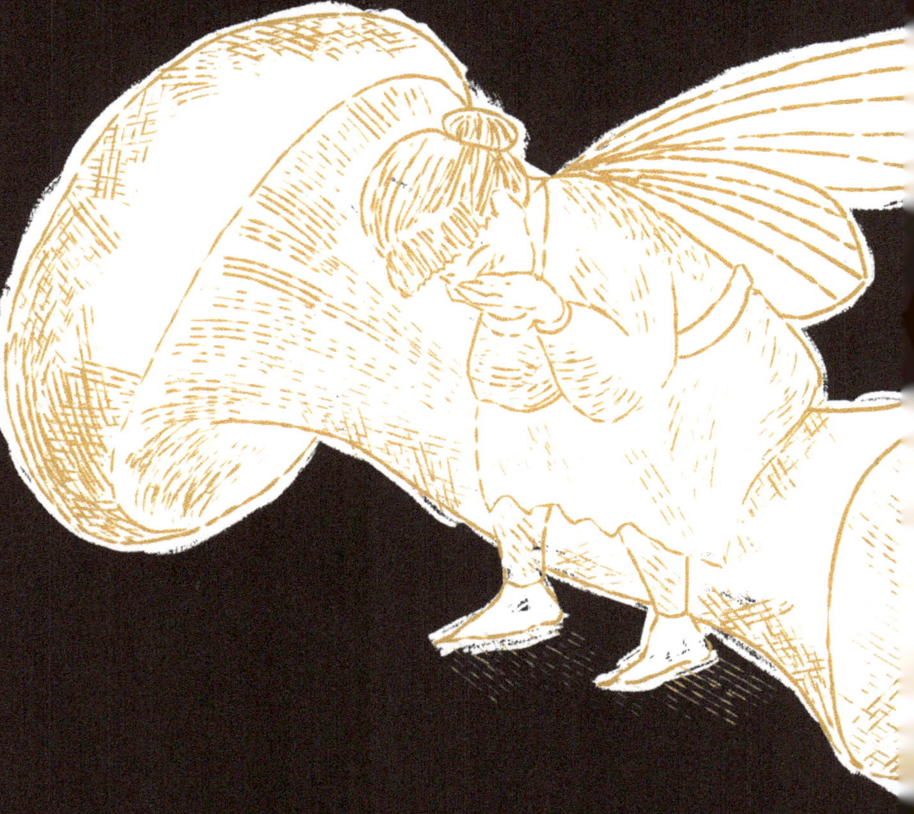

Chapter Six

ACTIVATING YOUR MIRACLE

I'm not ordinary. Miracles never are. If Pinocchio had been ordinary, he wouldn't have needed a miracle from the fairy that fateful night. But what would have happened if Geppetto had wished on the star, and the fairy wasn't feeling up for miracles that night? What if that morning, as she was bathing in fairy dust, she just didn't feel as "shimmery" as she once had? After all, the last two people she tried to help were complete failures. One of them woke up in the middle of her flying through their bedroom window and thought she was an intruder. She still has the bruises from the villagers' wife swatting her with a broom while chasing her around the dining room table and out the front door. Surely, she carries that kind of trauma with her into the next assignment. I wonder whether she ever felt "less special" or "less capable"? Did she approach every open window with the same vigor and awe at what was about to be accomplished? Did she ever feel just not quite up to it or as if the task was just too much for her?

I relate to the fairy because I've been in those moments when I had to choose to go from failure to failure without losing enthusiasm, so when the right window opened, I was ready for the miracle. During the early days of my entrepreneurial journey, Andrew and I were broke, but we were determined to persevere. Resolutely, I hit the pavement doing sales and cold calling businesses while driving my 1980s burgundy Ford Ranger that didn't have air conditioning in the heat of a southern summer. My strategy was to pick a community, park my Ford Ranger, and walk the streets cold calling businesses. I always wore a suit when I made sales calls and by the fourth call it would be drenched through with sweat. As soon as I entered a business, the response was always, "Oh my goodness. Let me get you some water." I'm convinced the only reason I got to do pitches was because of pity. But I remember being on my 40th call, soaking wet from sweat and exhausted, and I had to talk myself into not giving up. It sounded something like, "Listen, this is bigger than you. I promise this will pay off if you will just take one more step and knock on one more door." After the call, I would start the internal dialogue again, *one more door, one more door*. Did the fairy have this same dialogue in her mind? *One more window, don't give up. You were made for this*. We know she must have kept her spirits up, otherwise the story of Pinocchio would have ended quickly.

MARGINALIZING THE MIRACULOUS HAPPENS WHEN WE DON'T BRING OUR MIRACLE TO A SITUATION WHEN IT COULD BE THE THING THAT PIVOTS THE FUTURE OF ALL INVOLVED.

Marginalizing the miraculous happens when we don't bring our miracle to a situation when it could be the thing that pivots the future of all involved. This is what it looks like when we refuse to be "then it happened" people. The fastest way to marginalize the miraculous is to not recognize it, accept it, and access it in ourselves. Winston Churchill once said, "Success is going from failure to failure without losing enthusiasm," and that is exactly what the fairy did. The moment wasn't too big for her. She had no doubt she was made for this, and she knew on the other side of her involvement everything changed. We need to come to the same realization that everything changes after we get involved. Regardless of whether you feel like your involvement matters, the truth is that your involvement will change everything.

Truth isn't dependent upon anything other than itself, and it is never relative. If anything is relative, then it can't be true. For example, if I see something as true, but you don't, then we aren't arguing over truth, instead we are arguing over an opinion. All truth is immovable and unchanging and for everyone on the planet, when you get involved, everything changes because you bring perspective, attitude, and skills to the table that otherwise aren't present. However, your impact will be determined to the level your skills are developed, to the level your skills are deficient, and to the level of your attitude toward the cost of investing those skills. I'm confident that when I get involved, everything will change for the better because the net of teammates is always positive, and I know what I'm good at. We all have the capacity to activate the miraculous in ourselves and others, but to do this, we need recognition, acceptance, and access.

YOUR IMPACT WILL BE DETERMINED TO THE LEVEL YOUR SKILLS ARE DEVELOPED.

After Figaro opened the window, Geppetto immediately noticed the wishing star—the fairy. She could have dimmed her light to go unnoticed, but she didn't. Her light was brighter than all the other stars. Geppetto made his wish, and then it happened. The fairy recognized the opportunity for the miraculous to take place. When she flew through Geppetto's window, she brought her full self, made all of her resources available, solicited teammates to participate, built on what was already prepared, and created an environment where miracles weren't just possible, but probable. The fairy understood that no matter how many failures she had previously experienced, she was a "then it happened" fairy.

RECOGNITION

Recognition is always a question of assessment and inventory. Recognition says, "here's what I have," while inventory

RECOGNITION IS ALWAYS A QUESTION OF ASSESSMENT AND INVENTORY.

always answers the question, "how much do I have?" When we are honest about what we have and how much of it we are willing to part with, then we begin to understand what type of impact we can have on situations.

In Pinocchio, the fairy recognized Geppetto's deficit. She knew there was no way for him to get what he wanted by himself. Maybe the fairy considered the options for making Geppetto's miracle happen. Perhaps she smiled while she thought about all the single ladies she could make fall in love with Geppetto, or maybe she would make him younger so he would have a better chance at finding love and having a son, because by all accounts the fairy is not lacking power. But the fairy saw what Geppetto had already been working on, and she knew if she added to what Geppetto had already done, then she could get him to where he wanted to be. She created nothing new, and she didn't try to be the miracle; instead, she helped Geppetto produce one himself by recognizing what he already had—Pinocchio. Like the fairy, we can all activate the miraculous in others when we recognize we are a miracle.

Recognition and deficit go hand in hand. If you notice a leadership deficit in your company, then most likely you have the skills to help impact the situation, because we will recognize deficits we are purposed to impact. Maybe you notice deficiencies in the sales process at your company? If so, then most likely you have the answer inside of you for how to fix it, because what you notice indicates what is inside of you.

Nature hates a vacuum, so if you are shaped to fill the vacuum, then it will suck you in. If you are shaped to impact and bring change to a situation, noticing the deficit will suck you into the hole you are meant to fill. When I see a deficit in something or in an organization and I recognize how I can fulfill the deficit (my skills that match the issue), the way I take responsibility for that situation is acceptance.

ACCEPTANCE

I recognize there is something strangely unique about me; however, recognizing it and accepting it aren't the same thing. Acceptance is different from recognition because acceptance carries with it responsibility. Acceptance is the intrinsic understanding that I have these abilities to connect and cause change, but they are meant for others and are squandered if not used. Because of that mindset, I actively look for opportunities to engage and cause impact. For example, I can recognize the sun is out, but *accepting* the sun is out requires action and responsibility on my part. Accepting the sun is out requires me to put on sunscreen—I recognize the sun is out and now, through acceptance, I take responsibility for how I act or don't act.

Acceptance and responsibility are the same thing. When I see a deficit and I accept my part in bringing the miraculous, then I

RESPONSIBILITY IS OWNERSHIP IN ACTION.

> **ACCEPTANCE IS THE INTRINSIC UNDERSTANDING THAT I HAVE THESE ABILITIES TO CONNECT AND CAUSE CHANGE.**

have to take responsibility for the situation and the repercussions. Problem solving in the corporate world is about how to move your people from the recognition stage to the acceptance stage. In the corporate world, many people see a problem, which is recognition and understanding of the deficit, but then they simply move on. They might talk about the problem at the water cooler or bring it up in staff meetings, but recognizing the problem was the invitation for acceptance so they could change everything through their involvement. This is where the idea of ownership versus membership comes into play.

If I am a member at a gym and the treadmill breaks, I will simply tell the management. But if I am the owner of a gym and the treadmill breaks, then I have to fix it. The problem is my responsibility, and I can't simply complain to someone else. Responsibility is ownership in action. Many people are simply members of an organization or employees, and they don't take ownership. If I see a problem and I accept responsibility for solving it (realizing I'm the answer and I'm the miracle), then I need to make sure my skills are refined so I can solve the problem and bring the miracle.

Accepting responsibility means you have to do the work, and your skills must be deployed, so those skills had better be refined.

The fairy recognized the deficit in Geppetto, and she accepted responsibility for making the miracle happen. However, in her downtime, she was refining her skills. Most likely, she used her off time to practice swirling her wand and identifying skills and assets in other people. She immediately recognized Jiminy Cricket as a contributor, but what if she hadn't been working on her emotional IQ, and she ended up picking Figaro as Pinocchio's conscience instead? I don't think things would have turned out well for Pinocchio. I imagine the story may have ended the same night, because Figaro, in a jealous rage, led Pinocchio into the fireplace so there would be no competition for Geppetto's attention. But that's not what happened. Nobody noticed the wishing star during the day, which was her downtime, but when night came, she was prepared.

One way to determine which skills you need to refine is by determining which deficits or problems your miracle is designed to fix. For example, if you are feeling stuck in your corporate structure or organization, then you will need to follow these three steps to determine which skills you should refine:

1. What deficits or problems do you notice in your workplace?

2. Are you in a position to influence this situation?

3. What would need to happen for you to take responsibility for solving this problem?

Your answer to question number 3 will determine which skills you need to refine so you can get unstuck and bring the miracle.

During the downtime, Geppetto sharpened his wood-carving skills so he could produce his miracle Pinocchio. If he hadn't sharpened his tools and refined his wood-carving skills, then Pinocchio would have been a deficit mess. In the same way, you need to define the problem you are meant to solve and then you need to refine the skills you need to be the miracle that you are.

PERCEPTION

Before I entered the corporate structure of the Fortune 400 company, my business experience felt like a family buffet. Everything was casual, and we related to one another like a big, happy family. But after my company was acquired, and I came on staff to help manage the transition, I immediately realized there were areas in me that needed to be quickly refined. Fortunately, I had great people around me who had skills in areas I didn't, and I was candid with them about the areas where I was weak. I never felt intellectually inferior to them; however, I was keenly aware they had more experience than me, especially because of how young I was compared to them.

At this company, the people I worked with had spent years in business and finance, building their careers and working their way up in their relative companies, while I had only been an entrepreneur for four years because Andrew and I were quickly successful. My lack of experience compared to theirs was so substantial that even dinners with them were awkward. I was a small-town southern boy who was now surrounded by Ivy League elites, and while they didn't hang any stigmas over my head, I felt the chasm.

They were refined and knew the good wine to order or how to pair it with the right entrée, and they ordered foods I had never heard of. A sophisticated palate was not something I possessed, having grown up in a normal home eating Hamburger Helper. Whenever I went to dinner with my bosses and colleagues, I felt inferior and never knew what to order. I studied how they talked so I could learn the language and know how to communicate when we went to dinner, and another friend helped me try new and weird foods each time we went out for dinner. I was fortunate to be around people who let me refine my social skills so that when it was time for me to transition to identifying problems I could fix, the transition was smoother because now I was an equal.

In my new corporate structure, I had relational hiccups with people because of perception. It wasn't until someone told me I should care about perception that I realized this was a skill I needed to refine during my downtime. Until this point in my career, I was unaware of how limiting others' perspective of us can be and that their perception of us matters. I was blissfully unaware of how people perceived me, and I didn't realize how unpleasant I was to be around. Whether this is emotional IQ, perception matters.

One of my colleagues, Erica, helped me the most to understand that other people's perception of me mattered and that I needed to refine that perception. Erica and I were the closest in age, but the furthest apart in almost every other categorical sense. But through mutual respect, we could have conversations that challenged me while also helping me to understand her perspective more clearly. She helped me to refine my social perception by opening my eyes to how people's observations of me weren't helpful for my career goals.

I will be the first to admit, I'm a little brash, and maybe once or twice I've been called arrogant. However, in meetings, I didn't recognize how off-putting my confidence or brashness was until Erica pointed this out to me. She would tell me the times I said things that made me look like a jerk and she would tell me to stop, which helped me to refine my people skills during the downtime. Through her brutal honesty, Erica helped me to refine my skills and be miraculous. But brutal honesty from a distance is mean because it says I don't want to get to know you, I just want to insult you. Any feedback you have to hurl instead of hand is an insult. And if you threw the feedback, you know it's going to come in hot. But constructive criticism has to be handed to you. Erica took the time to build a friendship with me, and she valued me as a person, and as a result, I could receive her criticism and change by refining my self-awareness.

Perception opens the window. If the fairy would have arrived at Geppetto's house and the window had been closed, Geppetto would have been an eighth of an inch of glass away from his miracle. The fairy would have seen the gap, identified the deficit, and been willing to take responsibility, but it would have been for nothing because the window was closed. Managing other people's perception of you lets them know there is an open window for the miraculous to happen. Perception is self-awareness, and it helps others to know you are accessible to their miracle. A high level of self-awareness means you identify what is true about yourself while being honest about what other people believe to be true about you. People always receive on the level they perceive. Entry level self-awareness is identifying your strengths and weaknesses, likes and dislikes, but the next level of self-awareness is understanding how people perceive you. In the downtime, take an inventory of how those around you perceive you.

> ANY FEEDBACK YOU HAVE TO HURL INSTEAD OF HAND IS AN INSULT.

PRACTICING IN THE DOWNTIME

Early on after my company's acquisition, I noticed a deficit in an area I was superb at—spotting trends, being current on technology, being vision-focused, and solving complex problems. I asked if I could transition to what I was best at and where I could bring a miracle to bear in the deficit, I wanted to be the Senior Director of Business Development. The senior vice president liked my idea and agreed I was the best person for the job of business development and an in-house entrepreneur. I saw the deficit, and I recognized inside of me I had everything needed to fix it.

But what would have happened if, instead of speaking to the senior vice president, I stood around the water cooler talking about how in a perfect world I would get hired to do business development? Nothing—nothing would have happened, and the miracle wouldn't have taken place. It would be like the blue fairy noticing a pile of sticks named Pinocchio and knowing she could make a miracle happen, but instead she complained to the surrounding stars about how she hoped somehow it worked out for Geppetto. When I noticed the deficit, I did something about it. Responsibility requires action, and action requires refinement of your skills.

I grew more in the downtimes of my career than in any other season because I used this time to sharpen and refine my skills. I wasn't the CEO, but I grew my skills as a CEO. Leadership coach and author John Maxwell wrote, "Most people who want to get ahead do it backward. They think, 'I'll get a bigger job, then I'll learn how to be a leader.' But showing leadership skills is how you get the bigger job in the first place. Leadership isn't a position, it's a process." If you want to be a CEO or an executive, then you have

THE MOST **MISERABLE** PEOPLE IN LIFE AREN'T THE ONES GOING THROUGH **REFINEMENT,** THEY ARE THE ONES WHO ARE **FIGHTING IT.**

TRANSITIONAL SEASONS ARE ALWAYS AN OPPORTUNITY TO REFINE YOURSELF.

to refine your skills during the downtimes or in the between times.

You can't work on becoming a better catcher in the middle of a baseball game. The only way to refine your catching skill is in practice during the downtime. In the same way, you can't refine the perception you project during the acquisition. You have to do it during the off-time so you will be ready for your miracle. Transitional seasons are always an opportunity to refine yourself.

The truth about refinement is that you're going to get it no matter what, and either you will be in charge of it, or the world will be. The most miserable people in life aren't the ones going through refinement, they are the ones who are fighting it. Like Geppetto, the world is going to use sandpaper to refine you and take the rough edges off. Take charge of this process by deciding which things will be refined when and to which degree. Difficulties are coming whether or not you want them to, and it's up to you to prepare for them. The level to which you submit to refinement will dramatically reduce the pain when it happens. Hedge against those challenges now in the downtime.

ACCESS

Access is about deciding which teams your miracle attributes fit best with and creating relationships that generate access to the issues you were created to solve. Access can be a process

THE SPEED AT WHICH VULNERABILITY HAPPENS IS ABOUT THE QUALITY OF THE RELATIONSHIP, NOT THE QUALITY OF THE MIRACLE.

because allowing others into the places where we need a miracle requires vulnerability and the speed at which vulnerability happens is about the quality of the relationship, not the quality of the miracle. Early in this book, I talked about empathy being deployed as a strategy. Empathy is a powerful tool that allows me to connect with someone else's passion, but vulnerability is the reverse of this process.

Vulnerability allows people into my situation or to have access to me. While empathy empowers you to connect with someone else's passion, it must be connected to vulnerability. It doesn't matter how much impact you bring or how much of a "then it happened person" you are, if the recipient doesn't allow you access through vulnerability, then the impact will not happen. Anything of sustaining impact in the world has been a combination of empathy and vulnerability, which requires two people to meet together for impact. Every successful team is equal parts empathy and vulnerability, and the way you get vulnerability from someone else is by giving vulnerability to them.

Allowing others into the place where we need a miracle requires vulnerability. I wouldn't be where I am today without practicing vulnerability. I am a high achiever who is always aware of the scoreboard, but there was a time in my life when I outpaced the score board. Andrew and I had achieved a lot quickly, and there wasn't another battle to fight or a win to make. I didn't know what to do with myself without having a win or an achievement to chase, and as a result, I became clinically depressed. People around me knew something was different, but they didn't know exactly what I was struggling with. I didn't get the help I needed until the day I told Andrew what I was experiencing and what was happening inside of my mind.

Andrew was always capable of helping me, and nothing changed in that moment for Andrew when I told him how I was struggling. What changed was me. I decided to give him access to me through vulnerability. I gave Andrew access to engage his empathy on my behalf. Until the day I shared my struggle, Andrew recognized there was a problem, he knew there was a deficit in me, and he even offered to take responsibility for it by telling me multiple times to let him know if I ever needed to talk. But none of that mattered until I gave him access through vulnerability. Nothing happens if people don't let you in, and access is a process. For others to allow us into the place they most need a miracle requires vulnerability, and the speed at which vulnerability happens is about the quality of the relationship, not the quality of the miracle. So give relationships time for trust to grow.

Every successful leader and entrepreneur needs to recognize that their unique differences bring the magic, and your teammates will have different capacities for recognition, acceptance, and access. However, everyone will have a different bearing on the result, based on the level of access. Who is waiting on what you have so their miracle can happen? Don't wait any longer. Bring your miracle to the situation where it will have maximum impact. Don't marginalize the miraculous inside of you; instead, recognize it, accept it, and access it in yourself and others. Bring the miracle of who you are to bear on the situation you are in and pivot the future of all involved.

Chapter Seven

PROGRESSING YOUR MIRACLE THROUGH LEADERSHIP

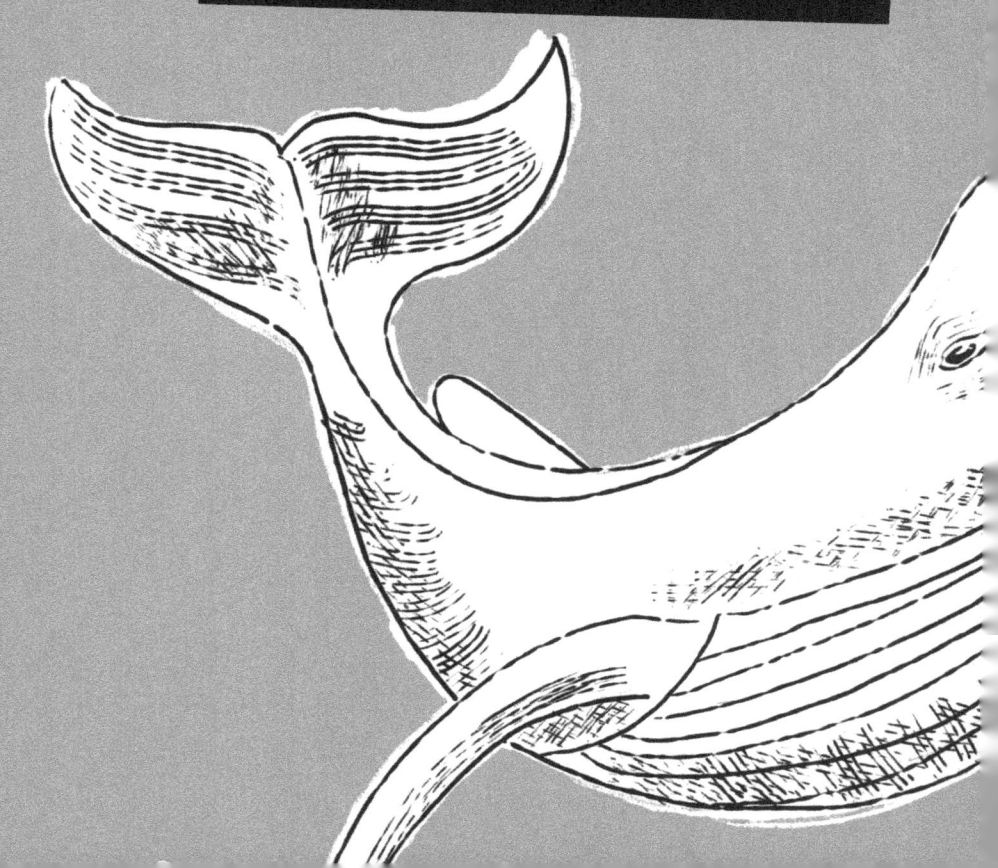

In the story of Pinocchio, Geppetto is the only person called to lead. He's the father with the natural position of leadership. The miracle of Pinocchio was Geppetto's dream. Jiminy Cricket wasn't sitting around thinking, *I wish I had a brat to babysit.* Jiminy Cricket's dream was food and a warm place to sleep. And Figaro definitely wasn't wanting competition for Geppetto's attention. In the story, everyone else is trying to figure out a way to either get rid of Pinocchio or how to profit off him, which isn't the care of someone who is responsible for a dream. One way to determine whether people are with you is to ask if they are trying to prevent or profit from your dream. If they are, then they are not with you. Being responsible for the progression of a dream is the only way to identify who the leader is.

Geppetto is the only one responsible for progressing Pinocchio. However, Geppetto repeatedly puts Pinocchio in situations where others try to profit off him and where Pinocchio hears other voices that he ultimately decides to believe and follow because Pinocchio wasn't ready for the real world. The one thing that would have protected Pinocchio in every scenario was his father's voice—the voice of the person responsible. If Geppetto had been there, would Pinocchio have missed school and ended up in a puppet show? No. Would Pinocchio have ended up on Pleasure Island if Geppetto had been there? No. If Geppetto had been there, would Pinocchio have ended up in the belly of a whale? No. Geppetto created multiple situations where his dream could have been ruined because he stayed home and made clocks, instead of speaking into the progression of his dream through leadership.

BEING RESPONSIBLE FOR THE PROGRESSION OF A DREAM IS THE ONLY WAY TO IDENTIFY WHO THE LEADER IS.

Doing what you have always done with excellence may give you a platform for your miracle to come. However, once you get your dream, doing what you have always done is the quickest way to watch other people steal it from you. The strategy for protecting your miracle is unique from the strategy of obtaining it. Once you have your dream, take responsibility for its progression. To take responsibility for your dream, you have to engage two strategies: frequency and volume.

FREQUENCY

In order to protect your miracle from the Honest Johns and Strombolis of the world, you need to activate a strategy I call frequency. Frequency means you consistently and repeatedly speak the final version of your dream to your people. If your people aren't hearing your voice often enough, they will follow any other voice that is giving direction. For Pinocchio, he wasn't finished—that's why he was sent to school. Similarly, as a leader, you have to continuously remind your people that the miracle isn't done and there is more to do. There is a quote I love from the movie, *The American President*, that says, "In the absence of leadership, the loudest voice wins." This is especially true in the corporate world. How often are your people hearing you speak of the vision and the dream? You need to be speaking often enough to drown out all the other voices who are vying for your position.

The way to measure if you are speaking enough is what I call "the law of overflow." Imagine I have a small glass of milk, which represents the person I am leading, and I have a jug of water that represents me as the leader. If I pour a little bit of water into the glass, will the milk be the same? No, because now it has an additive. I put something else into it. However, it wouldn't be enough water to tell the difference, so while it was different, it would still look the same. But now, imagine I pour the entire jug of water into the glass of milk until it overflows. Eventually, the milk would run clear. The new thing would displace the old thing. If the water coming out of me is my voice and what I am speaking, the vision from our company, I need to speak it often enough that it will overflow from the people I am leading. If I pour enough water, they will look just like me.

> FREQUENCY MEANS YOU CONSISTENTLY AND REPEATEDLY SPEAK THE FINAL VERSION OF YOUR DREAM TO YOUR PEOPLE.

TELL YOUR STORY

You can determine if you are pouring enough water, so to speak, by asking, "Are the people I'm leading saying what I'm saying? Are they speaking the vision I spoke into them? Are they able to parrot the vision?" My favorite assessment question is, "Do they know our story?" A great leader needs to tell their story every day. Walt Disney repeatedly painted magical things with his voice, and he was an incredible leader because he always told his story. He once said, "Leaders restore order with imagination." Walt verbalized his vision and people followed because they believed what he said was true, they believed what he said was possible, and they decided his voice was the one to follow. As a result, the people working for him bought into his rhetoric. He spoke what he believed often enough that it transformed his people.

GOOD, BETTER, BEST

In a good, better, best scenario, *good* is when you are constantly managing the amount of water in your jug because it is finite. But, in this scenario, you have to continuously refill your jug as a leader. This would look like going to conferences, regularly reading books on leadership, and having others pouring into you, then dumping out into your people. Then returning to get more information, which often changes, and bringing that back and dumping it out into your people again. The danger here is that it is easy to get perceived as a leader that is constantly shifting based on the last thing they read, or speaker they heard, and then shifting the vision around these new thoughts.

REGULARLY SPEAK VISION AND PURPOSE INTO THE PEOPLE YOU'RE LEADING.

In a *better* scenario, as a leader, you are connected to a source (like a hose). Leadership skills and growth are part of your lifestyle. In the better scenario, you have a changing and growing leadership mindset, and understanding and reading and growing as a leader is a regular part of who you are and your job, BUT your vision is steadfast and stays the same. For example, if your job as a CEO is to make widgets and you lead the teams that make widgets, your job isn't to make widgets; your job is to be the best leader of the widget makers. Making time to become a better leader is not part of the job, it's the whole job. Being connected to a source (making refinement a lifestyle) frees you up to focus on becoming a better leader while your team is focused on winning on the scoreboard.

The *best* scenario is when you are managing the overflow. This allows you to multiply the team wins exponentially. This happens when you put certain practices (managing the source) in your life where you know you are getting leadership built into you, so now you can focus on the overflow. This is what happens when you have a relationship with the people you are responsible for. If they are overflowing, you put more glasses (people) under them to catch the overflow. This is how you build a leadership organization where a relationship is the thing that exponentially grows the organization instead of relationship simply being the thing you have to do to transfer knowledge. As the leader, pour your words, vision , and story inside the people in your organization through relationships and allow them to do the same.

I regularly speak vision and purpose into the people I'm leading. No where is that more evident than my family. For example, as a father, I repeatedly speak life and vision into my kids. If you were to ask any of them who Daddy's favorite is, each of them would answer they are Daddy's favorite because I tell all three of them they are Daddy's favorite and I love them. When I hug my teenager and tell him I love him and he's my favorite, he replies, *I know.* This is the response all three of them give me because I've spoken this truth into them their whole life. My kids know their father loves them because I am always saying it. If you ask my daughter who she is, she will reply, *I am strong, smart, pretty, and brave.* She doesn't say, "Daddy says I'm strong, smart, pretty and brave," because that isn't owning it. She says, "I am strong, smart, pretty, and brave." She owns it as her identity, which is the overflow of the words I have spoken into her. Now she identifies as this. She has internalized this message of truth, and she has decided that what Daddy says is true and that my voice is the one to follow.

In a corporate setting, this looks like speaking the vision frequently enough that it overflows from your people. At one of my companies, our motto was "Serve first, sell second." In every business dealing with clients, we approached them with the attitude of, *How can we serve you?* We weren't focused on selling

YOU WILL KNOW IF YOU ARE TELLING YOUR VISION AND STORY FREQUENTLY ENOUGH WHEN IT OVERFLOWS FROM YOUR PEOPLE.

product; we were focused on serving. We would say things like, "Can we come and do leadership development for your staff? Is there something you need sponsored, because we will sponsor it? What can we do to serve you and your staff because we want to do it?" We weren't worried about our needs because our motto was to serve first. As a result, our company grew by leaps and bounds, and we were widely respected. Most importantly, clients loved our people. There was never an event they did not invite our company to. During trade shows or conferences, clients would seek us out simply to say hi and to give a hug. Even though we were selling software, we were connected to our clients because they experienced our attitude of serving and they knew we genuinely cared about them. Our clients became our friends because we served first and sold second.

The motto I wrote for my company was: "Customers will never love a company until the employees love it first. Lead with product, stand out with service. Make it work, then make it better. Always deliver more than expected." I believe this motto with all my heart, which is why I was intentional about helping my employees love our company. My people loved where they were positioned within the company, and they believed our motto of serve first, sell second. My people loved our clients, and they understood the value of serving. They knew the result would be that customers would love doing business with us because we loved our company. But my employees could only love the company as much as I loved it and as much as I shared the vision. This goes back to the law of overflow. You will know if you are telling your vision and story frequently enough when it overflows from your people. Frequently speak the final vision of your dream to your people and manage the overflow.

IF YOU HAVE A RESPONSIBILITY TO PROGRESS SOMETHING, THEN THERE WILL ALWAYS BE SOMEONE TRYING TO PREVENT IT OR PROFIT FROM IT.

VOLUME

To progress your miracle, a leader also needs to speak the vision loud enough, so their people hear it above all the other voices. This is my second strategy—volume. The idea of volume in a corporate setting is describing how loud something is. Many things can be loud, like colors, decor, merchandise, sounds, and attitudes. Loud is about how many of our senses a product or something engages.

> **LOUD IS ABOUT HOW MANY OF OUR SENSES A PRODUCT OR SOMETHING ENGAGES.**

How loud you will have to be with your vision depends on your team and how many other voices are vying to profit or prevent your miracle. Volume might look like putting your vision on shirts, on screen savers, or on the back of the bathroom stall doors, whatever it takes to engage the senses with your vision. Volume might even look like doing TED Talks on the vision, sending emails about the vision, groups texts about the vision, and celebrating when the team wins something regarding the vision.

As a leader or an entrepreneur, you need to understand that your approach isn't "I have to do this in case someone else wants to take over," because someone does. Instead, you have to say, "I have to do this because someone will always want to take over." Regarding your position as the leader, there will always be someone trying to take over your voice. Someone will always vie for your voice and your position of leadership, so you need to ask, "How many senses can I engage so I get all of their attention?"

In a family system, this looks like someone else vying for the position of speaking identity over my daughter. For example, society will always try to tell her what her value is, where to find it, and what products she needs to help her get there. This would be an example of someone, or in this case, culture, trying to profit from my vision, my miracle—my daughter. But they can't be allowed to be her voice because they aren't responsible for her progress. This is true of my sons. There will always be counterfeit voices trying to tell them what it means to be a man, but again, these other voices aren't responsible for my son's progress; they are just trying to profit off my miracle.

THE CONTRACT

I have to be speaking louder than all the voices trying to sabotage my efforts, and the same is true in the corporate world. If you have a responsibility to progress something, then there will always be someone trying to prevent it or profit from it. You can be a great leader who is full of empowerment and opportunity, but leadership is a contract that says, "I've promised to lead you well, and you've promised to follow." The way you make this promise is by deciding which voice is true—your voice or the one you are following. But the follower always has an opportunity to break the contract.

One of my companies was a closed system, and what I mean by that is the company functioned as a family, and we cohabitated in an open office. My software developers worked next to my salespeople who worked next to customer care and our lounge, where we hung out and played Ping-Pong. If I had a problem, I could stand in the middle of my office and see all the people who could fix it. While this closed system prevented office gossip, I still needed to speak our vision weekly and with volume. If I spoke the vision any less, then momentum slowed. This is especially important for CEOs or entrepreneurs who only have one town hall meeting a year. They aren't speaking the vision often enough or loud enough. You can't lead through vision this way, and other voices speaking louder and more frequently will profit from or prevent your miracle. Microsoft has a huge conference once a year with a high volume celebration, but they also do countless deployments throughout the year to speak vision to their people. The yearly celebration helps employees who are in a head-down type of setting.

I always strove to help my employees love where they worked. I made our workplace fun because I knew how much effort the job required. I had to bring the fun up to the same level as the hard work we had to do. The fun part or volume was a strategy for getting my voice heard. I could be a perfect leader but not get followed, because following is a decision based on whether your voice is true or perceived to be valid. You earn leadership by letting your people know you care about them. But you also need to make your workplace fun so your employees will have the energy they need to bring about the miraculous.

Fun is an issue of volume because it engages the senses. Fun validates the voice while drowning out all the other voices. The fun I instilled in our workplace reinforced that I cared about them. I needed to validate my voice with evidence that their needs mattered, and I valued them. Once my employees knew I cared and they believed my voice, it was easier for them to accept what I was saying was true and the more progress we made. Other companies will always vie for your people, but if you can get them to think, "I'll never find another place as fun as this," then your *volume validated* your voice and progressed your vision.

Tactically, fun mutes offers from anyone else.

THE BUS DRIVER

I liken leadership to the analogy of being a bus driver. A bus driver is responsible for the souls on board, and they have to make stops to let people on and off. Leadership comes with the understanding that not everyone is here for the entire journey and the final destination. As people come on and off, you have to understand how to adjust what you are doing for how many people you are responsible for and for where you are going. As the bus driver, you have to know the route, and you will need to let people on and off at different times.

Everyone on the bus has the same experience as the bus driver. They travel the same miles, in the same air conditioning, while listening to the same radio. They all have simple but slightly different seats, but everyone can still look out the window and see where they are going because they all have the same view or vision for where they are going. The only difference is that the bus driver is responsible for the route. He sees what is coming ahead, and he maintains the route. The bus driver is the only one with the responsibility of getting people to their destination. He is responsible for progress—for progressing the vision.

While no one else on the bus has the steering wheel or the responsibility for progress, they can work together to make the journey more pleasant. They can take responsibility by meeting needs such as providing snacks; someone else might sing songs to entertain the passengers; and maybe someone else might share a teaching. Everyone can bring their gifts to the bus to make the experience more pleasant for everyone, but ultimately if you get on the bus and the journey is pleasant but you only drive in circles

LEADERSHIP IS THE RESPONSIBILITY FOR GETTING PEOPLE TO WHERE THEY NEED TO BE—PROGRESSING THE MIRACULOUS.

and don't get to your destination, then you would be disappointed. If the bus driver didn't get you to your destination, then the journey was a failure. Leadership is the responsibility for getting people to where they need to be—progressing the miraculous.

I've always hated the quote that says, "It's not about the destination, it's about the journey." This quote supports the idea that value isn't the destination. Instead, it's about what you discover along the way, but I couldn't disagree more. Yes, the journey has value, but the point is the destination. The only people who feel like it's just about the journey don't have anywhere important to be. And people who don't have a destination are lost.

Great leaders don't wander through life; they have intentionality. But you can only have intentionality when you have a destination to progress your miracle toward. Wherever you are in your leadership journey, progress your vision by speaking it with frequency and volume. If your people aren't overflowing with the story of your company, then you need to share your story more. If your people are listening to other voices, then you need to speak with more volume. As the leader, it is your responsibility to progress the vision, so do it often and do it loud.

Chapter Eight

PREVENTING MUTINIES

Miracles are naturally easy to receive. For example, did Geppetto put forth any effort for his miracle? Yes, he did a substantial amount of work initially, but when the time came for the miracle to take place, Geppetto was asleep. The problem with miracles is they are also fragile and just as easily stolen. You may be doing a great deal of work to put yourself in position to receive your miracle, but if you aren't putting in the same amount of work to protect your miracle, then you are destined to have it stolen. You are one voice, but there are countless miracle thieves. Everyone has a voice, and if your one voice isn't present, then a thief will profit from or prevent your miracle.

Some of these voices may even be better than yours. For example, in the story of Pinocchio. Honest John was crafty. He was a fox for a reason. He started by saying, "I'm honest, John." Immediately, he put Pinocchio in a position to believe that what I have to say is true just by calling himself honest. The other voices surrounding your company or organization, or your competitors, are trying to convince the person who is crucial for your vision to come to pass that your voice is less valid than theirs. The moment this agreement is made between the counterfeit voice and your people that the counterfeit voice is more valid than yours, you have lost them.

Geppetto was acutely aware of the outside world and how his miracle was different, but he didn't change his strategy to match his reality.

He took the right information and made the wrong assessment. Yes, his miracle was moving forward, but sometimes we confuse movement with direction. The wind is in our face; we sense the acceleration, and we know the G-forces are pushing us back into our seats. We get a false positive of what we imagine to be the indicators of growth happening, but we aren't actually moving toward our miracle. Instead, we are driving in circles, or worse, empowering other voices, resulting in chaos.

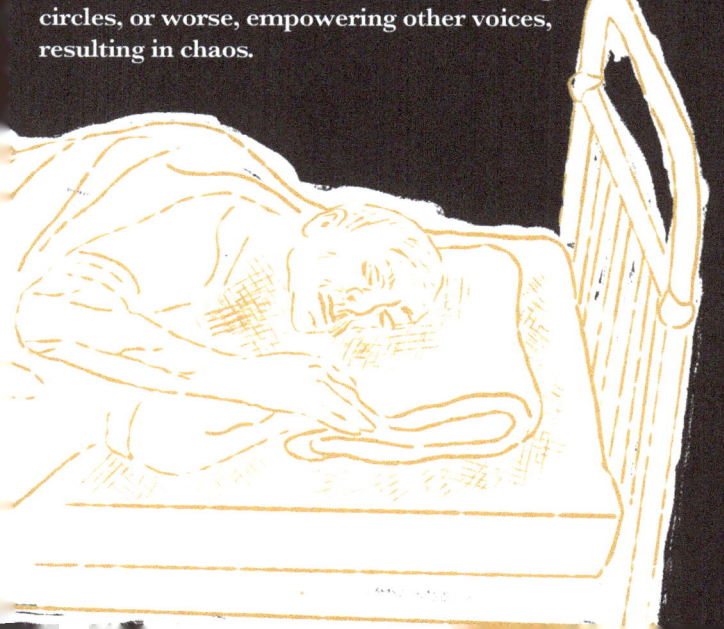

As the leader, you know the destination is the primary thing that matters, but what happens when you fail to tell your story often enough or loud enough? What happens when someone else convinces your people that their voice is the one to follow? Leaders always need to be ready for other people who will attempt mutinous power grabs. So whether you have lived through one or you want to know how to prevent one, start now to prevent leadership mutinies in your organization.

WHO'S FOLLOWING WHOM?

Leadership from the visionary perspective is opportunity and empowerment, but it looks different depending on whether you are leading as a leader or as a follower. From a follower's perspective, you can make a leader out of any voice you deem to be true. There are many people who will offer opportunity and empowerment, but as a follower, you have to decide who is going to be your leader. This happens when you agree that what they are saying is true. In a corporate structure, the leader will state the benchmarks that need to be met, and here is how we are going to do it. Then the followers have to decide to believe what the person in charge has said to do and then they can follow the leader in achieving the goal. You are being led the moment you decide what someone said is true. But when someone convinces your people their voice is the one to follow, then you have a mutiny on your hands.

A leadership mutiny happens when people in any organization

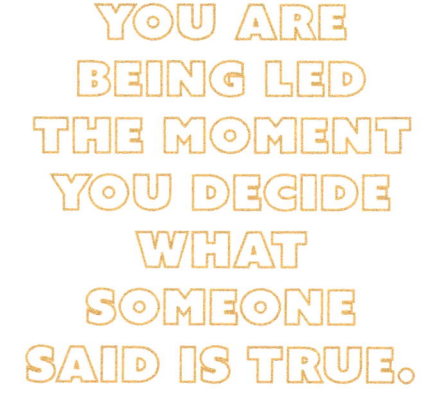

YOU ARE BEING LED THE MOMENT YOU DECIDE WHAT SOMEONE SAID IS TRUE.

decide to usurp the leadership in place. This can happen if the leader loses trust, abdicates responsibility, crumbles under the weight of leadership, or somehow disqualifies themselves through their actions. They still may have the position of leadership, and in the eyes of the people they are responsible; however, they have lost trust. In these situations, other people in the company or organization may decide to start leading without the actual position or authority of leadership. This is a leadership mutiny, and it can happen to anyone.

WHO HAS THEIR EAR?

A mutiny can come from anywhere in the organization and often catches the leader by surprise. Other voices will always try to convince your people that their voice is the one to follow, and the sign that tells you they are lost is that they stop saying what you are saying. There is no more overflow coming from them. If you want to know who has their ear and heart, listen to what they are saying. Next, find the person above them who is saying the same thing—map it backward.

In my new Director roll, I wasn't popular with one person on our executive team. However, I had to work with people on his team and while he managed to keep it cordial face to face, my team and I experienced a lot of negative attitude from the people that worked for him. Once his team pushed someone on my team to tears. I would not stand for this unprofessional behavior, and I confronted them and made them apologize. Interestingly, this person had no context for their attitude. As a support staff, this person was disconnected from the executive team with a limited context. They were speaking from a perspective that wasn't theirs because they didn't even know me or my team. This person was giving us attitude because it was the overflow of their boss.

A MUTINY CAN COME FROM ANYWHERE IN THE ORGANIZATION AND OFTEN CATCHES THE LEADER BY SURPRISE.

I could map it backward to see who they worked for so I could determine where the negative overflow was coming from. When you lose someone in your organization to another voice, you can map it back to discover who stole your voice—who stole your miracle. This is true in the reverse. On a higher level of leadership, you can discover who is disgruntled by finding out who under them is disgruntled because it flows down. The law of overflow works both ways, and when you identify this has happened in your organization, then you need to address the situation quickly.

Ninety percent of my time as a business consultant is spent helping people deal with leadership mutinies. Leadership mutinies are conditional, and your response will depend on where you are positioned within the organization, who is trying to mutiny, and how bad you let it get. The issues only worsen when mutinies are allowed to continue because the person in charge wasn't a great leader and they didn't address the issues. When this happens, the leader still has the position without having the people, and a position without the people is failed leadership.

THE LEADER STILL HAS THE POSITION WITHOUT HAVING THE PEOPLE, AND A POSITION WITHOUT THE PEOPLE IS FAILED LEADERSHIP.

LEADERSHIP VACUUM

While recovering and regaining people is always the same process, tactically it is different. For example, you become a leader by everyone deciding your voice is true, and you empower people and give them opportunity, but you are in a mutiny when you don't have people deciding to follow you anymore because they have decided that another voice is true. If you are experiencing a leadership mutiny, you need to determine which scenario you are dealing with. One question you might consider is what are your people trying to get by following this other voice? The other voice may not be in a position to provide empowerment or opportunity, which means they are not functionally able to lead, but they may have the loudest voice. When things are not going well in an organization or a company, then criticism looks like leadership. The critical voice is able to critique without giving empowerment or opportunity. If the dissenting voice is not able to lead, it creates a leadership vacuum.

WHEN YOU LOSE SOMEONE IN YOUR ORGANIZATION TO ANOTHER VOICE, YOU CAN MAP IT BACK TO DISCOVER WHO STOLE YOUR VOICE—WHO STOLE YOUR MIRACLE.

If you, as the leader abdicated responsibility and didn't lead, and the other voice positionally can't lead, then you have a vacuum of leadership, which is total chaos. Chaos and anarchy never move an organization forward, and progress is stopped. As a leader, you won't be able to address anything until you bring order within your organization. Walt Disney said, "We restore order with imagination." As a leader, imagine a better future for your people and for your company. Return to square one and evaluate what a perfect organization or company looks like or smells like. Begin again with the question, "How do I make a miracle happen?" What would it look like if you were in control again, doing a good job, your people trusted you, and you had their hearts and ears? Then craft a new story around that vision because your old story is shot. If you are living in the middle of a mutiny, then you have to start over.

NIPPING A MUTINY

I've never had to live through a mutiny. I've seen it tried a few times, but it didn't get far because I quickly restored order. One example of this is during a time when a set of employees tried to mutiny. My company had a well-established culture, and I had a strategic system for new hires that I always deployed except in this situation. Against my better judgment, I usurped my own process I had established for two new hires. My process was that new hires would meet with me first, which is when I would give them the vision of what we wanted to do. This wasn't a time for me to get to know them, it was a time for them to understand who I was and how I operated.

The potential hire then would interview with our COO, Kevin, who was the person doing the hiring. Kevin would tell the potential hire that I was the voice the company listened to and followed, and while we worked hard, we played hard, too. After Kevin told them the skills required for the job, we randomly selected an employee to interview them. The only part of the process I cared about was whether the employee thought this person would be a good fit for our company. I knew I could train skills, but what I didn't know was whether the person would be a good fit for our culture. And in hiring "Derek" and "Emily", I usurped my process. I didn't ensure they would fit our culture, and they didn't.

Derek was the new husband to a friend of mine, and he was having trouble finding work, so I told him he could come work for us. I showed up at the office one day and introduced Derek and told the staff he worked for us now. Little did I know, Derek was lazy, rebellious, and he took advantage of our friendship and my friendship with his wife. This would play out in the way he would intentionally avoid work by saying, "I'll have to talk to Tommy about that," before doing the work required of him. Even though I didn't let him get away with this part of his laziness, he would still attempt to usurp authority. When I confronted the situation by affirming to him he worked for Kevin, and not me, he became angry and cancerous to our organization.

Also, during this time I hired Emily during a season we were particularly busy, and she didn't go through our process either. Initially, she seemed like a good fit, but once she and Derek connected, the two of them started to corrupt other people in the organization. Eventually, some people began complaining about special privileges and anything they felt was inequitable. When I began hearing murmurs in the office, I knew exactly where it was coming from, and I knew I needed to nullify the mutiny quickly.

I ended up bringing those two plus one more employee into my office, and I told them that none of them were meant to be here. I told them they would be happier chasing their dreams.

I explained that they had dreams and passions they wanted to pursue, but they couldn't because they were here working for a dream that wasn't theirs. Derek wanted to have his own photography company shop, Emily wanted to help her husband with his business, and the other employee wanted to write children's books. I explained that I wasn't firing them; however, I believed in them, and I wanted to support them in their pursuit of their dreams. I wanted to do anything I could to help them achieve their passion.

So I made them all an offer.

I offered them 30 days paid time out of my pocket, where they could use the time to pursue their dreams, but at the end of the 30 days they could not come back to work for me if they took the offer. I also told them they had until the end of the workday to decide whether they would accept my offer to invest in their dream. However, if they decided not to take my offer, then I needed them to change their dream so they could pursue the collective dream of the company. This was a one-shot offer. Two of them returned from lunch with their decision to take my offer, and the third person stayed (although they quit after one month). None of these people ultimately pursued their dream, but I was able to rid our company of their toxic attitudes while also stopping a mutiny in a way that was caring and supportive. I restored order and eliminated chaos—mutiny averted.

REFUSING TO MUTINY

My great grandma always said, "Plain talk leads to a clear understanding," and this is how I operate as a leader and an entrepreneur. If you are a leader currently experiencing a mutiny, you need to understand that it is about doing the right thing

THERE IS NO HONOR IN MUTINIES, AND THE CURRENCY OF THE WORLD IS HONOR.

louder than the people doing the wrong things. As a follower, you can prevent a mutiny by refusing to usurp the person in the position of leadership. Two visions, by definition, is division. When the person who has the position of leadership loses their voice through abdication, lack of trust, or loss of vision, then a leadership vacuum takes place.

If people decide your voice is no longer true and no one else is speaking, then a vacuum of leadership results, and nature hates a vacuum. The vacuum will suck in a person the moment they give voice to fill the vacuum. People will follow that voice even if it isn't a good voice simply because they are averse to the feeling of a vacuum.

Being in a vacuum is uncomfortable and uninhabitable. People will champion anything that will plug the void. But it is a testament of character to not fill the leadership vacuum when you don't have the position of leadership. Very few people can do this. What you do instead is encourage the leader. You can encourage the leader to spill over more vision by letting them know there is a lack of vision, and you want the company to thrive under their leadership. You can coach and encourage your leader from the middle, but you can't lead from the middle. You can call out a vacuum without trying to fill it. In the corporate world, other voices will tell you to grab that moment to show your qualities, but that is devoid of integrity—it's a leadership mutiny. And it is the quickest way to get fired.

For example, if I'm a leader by position and you're a leader by mutiny, I can contain the mutiny by getting rid of you. In other situations, people assume they are being helpful, and this sounds like, "Well you weren't leading, so I led in order to get progress." But the reality is, whether or not it was helpful to the vision, a mutiny is a mutiny. If I'm in the navy and we mutiny and take over the captain's role, but we sail the ship into safe harbor, the navy will not congratulate me for sailing the ship. It's still a mutiny, and I'm going to jail. At this point, the destination becomes secondary. There is no honor in mutinies, and the currency of the world is honor.

PLAIN TALK LEADS TO A CLEAR UNDERSTANDING.

MUTINY ON THE BUS

In the same way the bus driver analogy helps us to understand how leadership progresses the miraculous, the bus driver analogy also helps us to understand what happens when there is a leadership vacuum. Leadership is the responsibility for getting people to where they need to be, which is what the bus driver does. However, consider how dangerous it would be if you gave everyone a steering wheel. The moment you give someone else a voice in your organization, it's like giving them another steering wheel. This is why mutinies have to be prevented. The moment you introduce two steering wheels into the situation, there is division. Two steering

ABOVE ALL ELSE, COMMIT TO THE PROCESS OF LEADING AND STEWARDING YOUR DREAM.

wheels can split a bus in half, but imagine what four or five steering wheels would do? This would look like blowing out the tires because someone was braking while someone else was pushing the gas. The transmission would be ruined because one person would want to go faster than another while arguing over the gearshift.

There can only be one bus driver. It doesn't matter how many snacks you have or how pleasant the journey is. The only true measurement of success is whether the bus makes it to the destination and if no one else has to think about driving the bus. The moment the bus wrecks, no one cares about how good the snacks were or how nice the music was or how pleasant the temperature was. When the community wrecks, everyone just feels the pain of the wreck—the mutiny. While getting cared for at the hospital after the wreck, no one will think about anything other than why Bill grabbed and jerked the steering wheel, causing the wreck.

The miracle is what you are driving, and you can't let multiple people steer it. If Geppetto's job was a bus driver instead of a clockmaker, then he would have been in charge of getting everyone in the story to where they needed to be. He would have put Pinocchio next to him, he would drive around the city and, before dropping Pinocchio off at school, Geppetto would have informed Pinocchio of the danger to avoid. Then Pinocchio would never have met Honest John because the bus route wouldn't have taken him that way. Geppetto would have gotten the bus where it needed to be while training Pinocchio on how to navigate the city and not marginalize his miracle.

If Geppetto was driving the bus, he would have made Jiminy Cricket walk the route, and he would have been a lot more involved in managing his miracle. But instead, it was like Geppetto pulled up to the first stop and said to someone random, "Hey, I'm going to take a nap in the back. You can drive the bus wherever you want." But that guy did not know how to operate a bus, and the next thing you know is that they are in the bad part of town. While Geppetto sleeps, Pinocchio is being led somewhere he isn't supposed to be.

Geppetto isn't thinking about Pinocchio. He is completely unaware of what is happening to this thing he has wished for—his miracle. This is how many people act when they get the miraculous. But if I said you could have your miracle if you will consistently do these steps, then I guarantee you would do the steps. The problem isn't getting your miracle, because that is the straightforward part. Progressing your miracle and protecting it from miracle thieves is the hard part, and it takes work. When people understand the difficulty level, they rethink their dreams because the work is in the miracle's progression—driving the bus and not sharing the steering wheel.

Are you ready for the work required to progress your miracle? If you are, then you need to protect it from miracle thieves and mutinies. And above all else, commit to the process of leading and stewarding your dream. You can plant a seed in a day. In fact, I could plant an entire field of corn in a day, and if I do nothing for four months, I'm going to get corn. But I won't be prepared for the harvest because all the work is done during the between times. Geppetto didn't understand this. He received his miracle in a seed form—a little boy made of wood. He didn't understand that he had work to do in the process for his dream to come to pass.

Wherever you are on your bus route, prevent future mutinies and regain current ones by taking a firm hold of your steering wheel

> PROGRESSING YOUR MIRACLE AND PROTECTING IT FROM MIRACLE THIEVES IS THE HARD PART, AND IT TAKES WORK.

and making sure no one else is calling out directions. If you have already experienced a mutiny, you can start again by regaining trust and gathering the right of followship. Take the time to do the work and to establish a new vision through storytelling. Every day a leader needs to speak vision and tell their story. Progress your miracle and do the work to protect it.

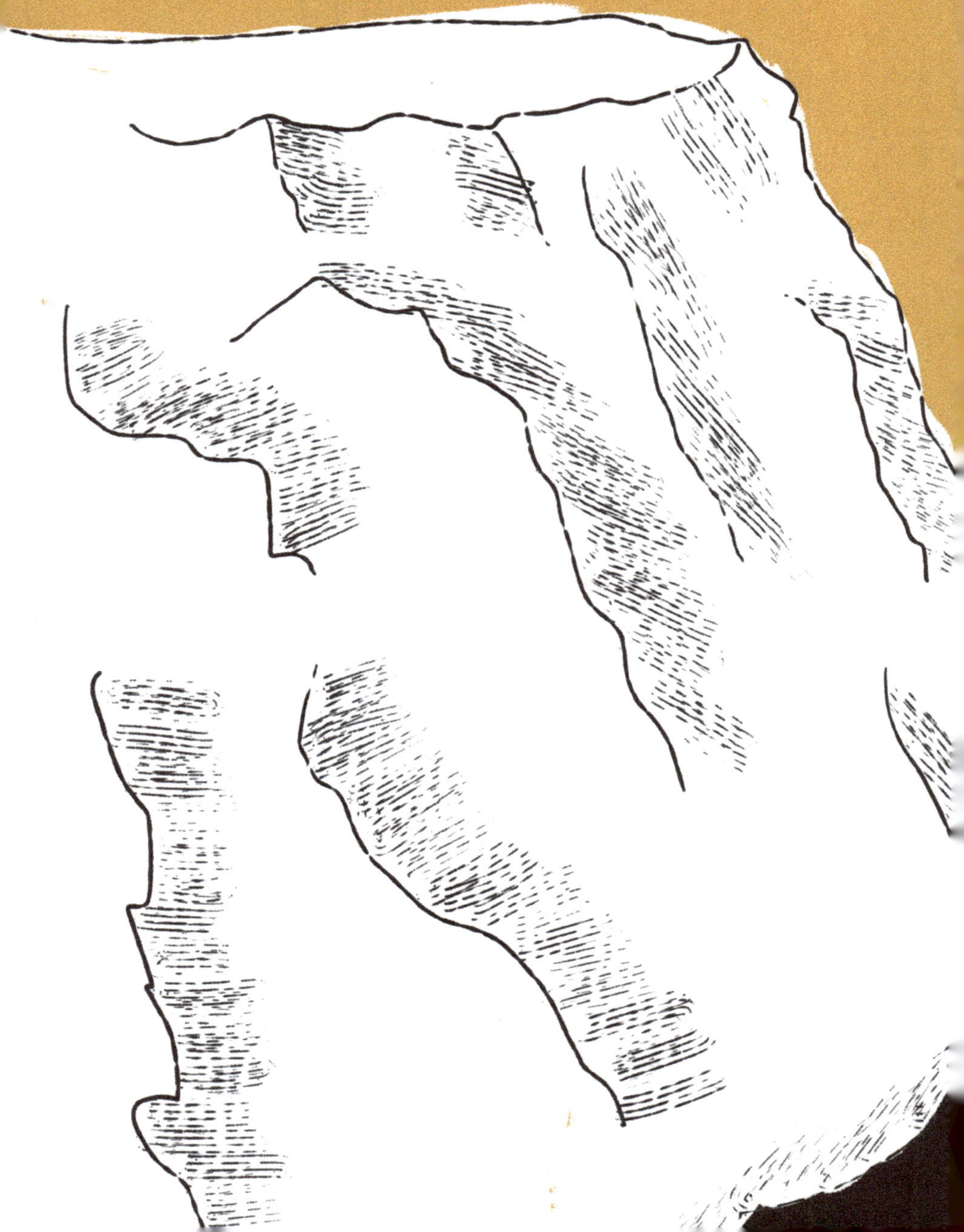

Chapter Nine

COUNTING THE COST OF THE RISK WORTH TAKING

In the ending scenes of Pinocchio, the miraculous is close to destruction on Pleasure Island. Unknown to Pinocchio, his selfish desires have taken hold and distorted the dream of what he was meant to be. At the last moment, Jiminy Cricket discovers that the boys on Pleasure Island are being transformed into donkeys. Jiminy rushed to warn Pinocchio just as a donkey's tail and ears sprouted from Pinocchio's wooden body. Was it too late? Had the curse taken hold of Pinocchio, destroying his future hopes of being a real boy? Just as this thought flashed through our minds, Jiminy shouted for Pinocchio to follow him to the only escape route possible. As the two race toward their freedom, they end up standing on the jagged edge of a cliff. Standing on the brink of complete annihilation, Pinocchio and Jiminy are forced to make a choice. Do they risk jumping into the dark abyss of the ocean, or do they return to the torment and distortion of Pleasure Island? They count the cost and decide jumping into the unknown is a risk worth taking.

We hold our breath. Moments pass, and we discover the risk paid off. The two pull themselves ashore to safety.

THE RISK WORTH TAKING

Every leader or entrepreneur faces risk. It's the bridge all must cross if they want to blaze a trail. But for most entrepreneurs, the risk is exhilarating. Most entrepreneurs may not even realize they are taking a risk because it feels riskier not to move forward toward their miracle. This is what sets them apart from managers.

> EVERY LEADER OR ENTREPRENEUR FACES RISK. IT'S THE BRIDGE ALL MUST CROSS IF THEY WANT TO BLAZE A TRAIL.

Managers focus on doing things right, but leaders focus on doing the right things and taking the right risks. Managers are given a set of circumstances and told to find success within those circumstances. But that's not good enough to qualify for leadership. Entrepreneurs or leaders want to have a set of circumstances where they get to figure out what the right steps are to take and, sometimes, which confines to avoid.

For the manager, risk taking is terrifying and something to be avoided. Entrepreneurs hate to manage, but they love to take risks. They are ready to start a fire in the whale's belly to see what will happen, even if it means total failure. The risk for them is worth it to move forward. Risk is not without the possibility of failure, and just because you may experience failure doesn't make you a failure—it makes you a risk taker.

For some, failure is a deterrent for trying again, but I think the opposite is true. For me, living through failures, ideas that didn't work, or businesses that dissolved, inoculated me to the fear of failure. In retrospect, I see how I survived failed attempts or risks that didn't materialize, and not only did I survive, but I came out stronger and more experienced. But here's the problem: Progress is emotional, and when you are rising after a failure or when you are trying to avoid one, your emotional state is directly linked to your progress. Your emotion will keep you going even when you are facing a potential failure or recovering from one. Emotions also keep you learning as you create your strategy for the tactical part. You can fail at execution, but still continue forward if you feel good about it. However, if you fail in the emotional part of the risk, then you will be too fragile to face the challenges.

It is essential that the risk-taking entrepreneur maintain and protect a healthy emotional mindset. But what happens when you experience criticism or a missed expectation? Do you crumble under the pressure? No. You pick yourself up again and reframe the experience. You can learn something from everything if you are open to it. Some of the best wins for the entrepreneur were lessons learned by either their failures or by watching someone else's failure.

> JUST BECAUSE YOU MAY EXPERIENCE FAILURE DOESN'T MAKE YOU A FAILURE— IT MAKES YOU A RISK TAKER.

There is a quote I love from Napoleon that says, "The role of the leader is to define reality and give hope." As the entrepreneur, leader, or CEO, you need to accept truth, resist denial, and protect your emotional perception at the same time for success. And while this may seem like a tall order, practice makes progress. Yes, you will have setbacks, and that's okay. Setbacks don't equal failure. If anything, they equal progress if you handle them correctly because now you are more knowledgeable than you were before. Failure increases your level of experience more profoundly, even more than success sometimes does. Failure is a risk worth taking. It was for Pinocchio, and it will be for you.

WEIGHING THE COST

Pinocchio was completely unaware that Geppetto had been searching for him. In fact, he took a boat onto the same waters Pinocchio just pulled himself from in an attempt to find Pinocchio. Not only was Geppetto lost at sea, but he was swallowed whole by the fearsome whale, Monstro. Determined to rescue his father, Pinocchio searched the ocean and let himself be swallowed by the beast so he could find Geppetto. This would cost Pinocchio a great deal, and maybe even his life, but he weighed the cost and decided the risk-to-gain ratio was worth it.

Everything in life has a cost—no exception. As a leader, it is your job to determine the cost and to decide whether it's worth it. When I'm talking about cost, however, I'm not talking about money. I'm talking about time. Time is the only currency that exists in the world. Ultimately, you are trading your life for anything you trade your time for. If someone were to ask you if you would give your life for your house or your dog, most likely you would say no; however, that is exactly what you do every day. You go to work for eight hours a day to get money to pay for your house and to have money to buy food for your dog. You gave your life to your house and dog because you gave your time. Every currency on the planet is based on a trade for someone else's time, and everyone has the same amount of wealth because everyone gets the same 24 hours every day. In determining access and where you are going to give your miracle away, there is an "opportunity cost" to consider.

Opportunity cost is an everyday term for any business. In my first business, trade shows were everything, but they were also expensive, so when we did a trade show, we counted the cost. We figured out how many sales we needed to make to pay for the show and then clearly communicated our expectations to our sales team. Every time they hit the mark. But we were clear about our goals and our costs, and we were always managing opportunity costs.

My time is limited, and there are only so many businesses I can run. I have said "no" three times more than I have said "yes" to projects because I understand opportunity cost. At this point in my career, any increase of opportunity will cost my family, and I owe them time first. I also have to evaluate the outcome. Recently, I was in a season where I took on an opportunity that required late nights and long hours, but after evaluating the outcome, I decided it was of value to me. I had stock in this company, and by staying on with them for almost two years, the value of my stock would drastically increase. I counted the cost to gain ratios.

> EVERYTHING IN LIFE HAS A COST—NO EXCEPTION.

Also, when determining what to say "yes" to, I ask, "What is it going to cost them if I don't get involved, and am I willing to let them eat that cost?" I know if I get involved, everything will change exponentially, and I know if I don't get involved, everything will change. Ask, what is the cost on both ends? In business, change is the only constant. However, to help me navigate that change, I have five non-negotiables when considering opportunity cost:

» Is this opportunity going to violate a trust I've already established?

» Do I want to do this?

» What is the ROI (return on my investment)?

» Is there potential for more opportunity on the other side of this opportunity?

» What will happen if I don't, and am I okay with that outcome?

I don't manage my decisions on a cost basis. If I can bring a massive impact to a situation and it will not violate my non-negotiables, then it doesn't matter what it costs. For example, if you had an opportunity to buy a business that you knew was going to return 20 percent year over year, and they want ten million dollars, but you only have one million in your budget, you would need to find a way to finance that purchase. You need to make that purchase because the return is what determines the value. If I know I'm going to get 20 percent year after year, then I know I'm going to get all my money back in five years, which means every year after that I'm going to make two million dollars a year. Figure out a way to make the purchase, because it would be a smart business decision. The intelligent part of a business decision is not in the cost, it's in the return. If I want to do it, it

THERE IS AN OPPORTUNITY COST FOR INSTALLING THE MIRACLE, AND THAT COST IS ACCESS.

doesn't violate my trust, and the return is right, then I will figure out the cost. I will figure out how to finance my time and partner with someone else to get more time for greater impact.

I'm consulting with a business right now for free, and because the person running the business is a friend, he has what I call "relational access to me," and I know I can help. John knows that if he calls, I'm going to answer, and I know the same is true for him. However, the time I give to his company eliminates an unlimited list of things I could do that would either make me happy or make me money because I said "yes" to training his team. The opportunity to consult with this business has a cost because I can only do one thing at a time.

In the same way, Geppetto's miracle cost the fairy her impact. When the blue fairy came to Geppetto's window to answer his wish, no other wishes were granted that night. She couldn't visit anyone else's window. Who knows if someone in the village had a family member with smallpox and they made a wish that night for this family member to be healed, but in the morning, that family member still had smallpox? There is an opportunity cost for installing the miracle, and that cost is access. If you have access to me, that means someone else doesn't.

PIVOTING YOUR MIRACLE

In the belly of the whale, the two embrace. Geppetto is resolved to embrace a doomed fate, but not Pinocchio. As Pinocchio looks around, he quickly devises a plan. The miracle is now creating the opportunity for another miracle to take place. And while Geppetto was once the one positioned to rescue Pinocchio, now the tables have turned. In his defeated place in the whale's belly, Geppetto has lost all hope. He has given himself over to despair. But now it is Pinocchio's turn to make a miracle. And he does. Through innovation, he deploys his plan and executes a miracle to save Geppetto and himself in the process. It was a risk worth taking. The miracle rescues its creator. Pinocchio counted the cost and chose the risk. In the same way, every entrepreneur will continually face situations where you will need to count the cost or consider when it's time to risk, or like in this situation with Pinocchio, if it's time to let your miracle pivot.

Geppetto's miracle was going alright in the beginning, and Geppetto felt like it was business as usual, but then things changed. Slowly at first, but ultimately, things couldn't remain the way they were. Making a fire in the belly of a whale was a risk, but it was a risk that changed the outcome for everyone involved. Geppetto allowed his miracle to pivot so he could be rescued from Monstro.

WITHOUT EXCEPTION, EVERY ENTREPRENEUR WILL FACE A SEASON IN THEIR LIFE WHEN THEY NEED TO EITHER PIVOT THEIR MIRACLE OR LET THEIR MIRACLE PIVOT THEM.

Every entrepreneur dreams of being successful and having their miracle become a reality, but when it doesn't, what do you do? Do you stay in a house that caught on fire, while telling everyone else you're fine and the flames will go out? Or, like Geppetto, do you sit on your boat and make the best of it by spending your days catching fish and eating by candlelight with your cat and goldfish while in the belly of a whale? Without exception, every entrepreneur will face a season in their life when they need to either pivot their miracle or let their miracle pivot them. This is what Geppetto did. Things weren't working anymore. Geppetto's plans had failed, and he could either die with them or pivot.

To pivot simply means you change course. If you were headed in one direction, you strategically set your GPS and head in a different direction. And while this seems simple, it is not, because your emotions will inevitably be involved and your emotions are connected to your progress. If you are in a place where what you have been doing isn't working anymore, then determine what it is about what you currently do that you enjoy. What gets you excited to get out of bed in the morning? Once you've defined this for yourself, draw from the wisdom of people in your life who can speak encouragement into your new dream and who can offer you guidance when needed, because we are better when we are collaborating with others.

There is an ancient proverb that I love: "Where no counsel is, the people fall; but in the multitude of counselors there is safety." If you are miserable doing what you are doing, then pivot—change course. Draw from the wisdom of people around you and make a new plan. Yes, this feels risky, but remember who you are. You are an entrepreneur. You are the fabric of what makes innovative ideas work and thrive. You are how new business ideas succeed. Will there be a cost? Yes, but it will be worth it. Is there a risk? Of course, because every great entrepreneur needs a risk they can take. And after all, you are a risk worth taking, so light the fire in the belly of the whale and watch what happens when your miracle pivots you.

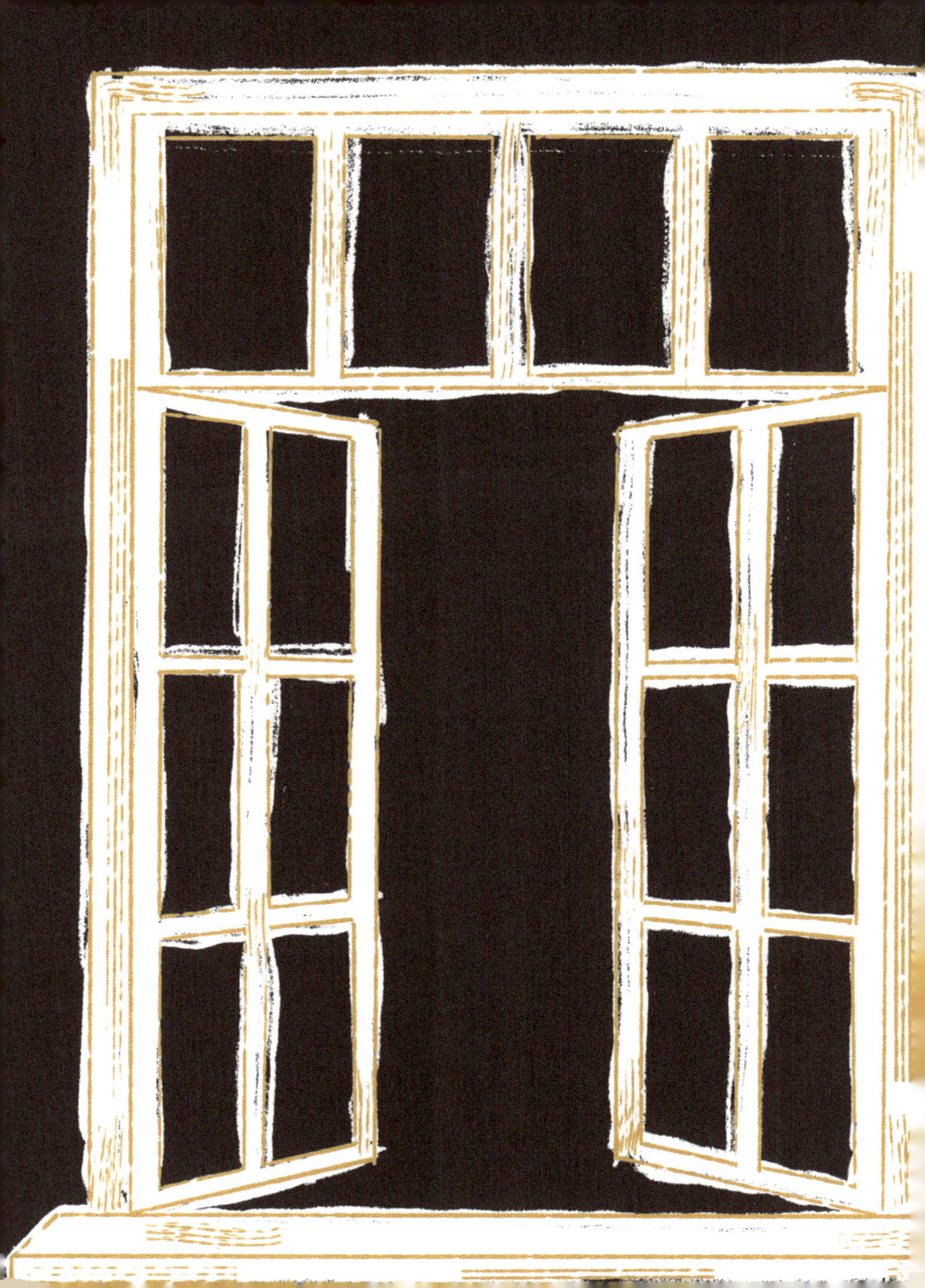

Chapter Ten

DREAMS REALLY DO COME TRUE

As the story of Pinocchio comes to an end, a bright light appears, and the fairy encourages Pinocchio to always be brave, honest, and unselfish so his dream will come true. Whatever your dream is, you are going to have to prove yourself, and you are going to need to do the hard work required to obtain it, because everything has a process. In the story of Pinocchio, the only ones who didn't work were the ones who received nothing—Figaro and Cleo. They remained bystanders the entire movie, and in the end, nothing was different. You can avoid the work like they did and choose not to harvest success, but like Figaro and Cleo, it will leave you forever dependent on someone else's success to provide for you. That's no way to live.

As the story comes full circle and we are once again staring at the starry sky through Geppetto's window, Jiminy jumps up onto the windowsill, opens the window, and looks up. Suddenly a solid gold-badge appears on his coat. He just received a major promotion. Jiminy Cricket is now the "Official Conscience"—of what we don't know, but he is glad just the same. All that running around chasing after Pinocchio and rescuing him from "Donkey Island" has paid off, and he has received a huge upgrade.

Everyone who wants to accomplish anything is going to have to work for it—no exception, because you can't hack growth. And if you don't do the work, then your days will be spent swimming in circles in a fishbowl, going nowhere fast. Nobody wants that. If you are still unsure what your miracle is, then take time to identify it. Consider what makes you unique and what stirs your passion.

Once you have identified your miracle, then follow these steps:

- » Put your miracle into motion.
- » Protect your miracle from normal.
- » Engage excellence as a strategy.
- » Progress your miracle forward.
- » Protect your miracle from mutinies.
- » Commit your miracle to the process.
- » Never give in to doubt.

For some people the hardest part of being a miracle is committing to the process—the growth—because it takes work. But don't let that discourage you. You've made it this far. Maintaining your miracle is worth it. And the more you deploy the necessary tactics for maintaining your miracle, the more they will become habits in your life, and you will be able to activate them automatically, because ultimately, the miraculous will change you and everyone around you if correctly deployed.

YOU CAN'T HACK GROWTH

Have you ever heard the cliché, "If you love what you do, you will never work another day in your life"? I couldn't disagree more with this expression, because work is work. Yes, it can be fun, but it's hard and challenging. Many want to find a career that feels like vacation, and maybe this is because they grew up hearing that the American Dream was to retire one day and stop working. But I think this is a distortion of reality that leaves us thinking subconsciously that the American Dream is *to not work*. The idea in this scenario is, *Get to a place where you have accumulated so much wealth where you don't have to work anymore*. The problem with this way of thinking is that it makes work the enemy. Instead of work being something I enjoy and that I am passionate about, now work is something I have to tolerate until I stop doing it and retire.

In contrast, we can have the approach of, *This is something I get to do*. There are millions of people around the world who don't have access to work that will provide for them and grow their lives. Yet here we are trying to hack growth, avoid the process, and skip to the end of our American Dream so we can do nothing. But what if you decided to enjoy the process while doing the work? Not only does the process bring refinement to your life and others, but it makes you a better person.

SUCCESS IS MEANT TO BE A PROCESS, SO TRYING TO HACK IT IS A WASTE OF TIME.

Those close to me know that I love Mondays. Believe it or not, it's vacations that I'm not a huge fan of. I love what I do; consequently, I love to work. I realize I can't hack growth, so I put in the work to maintain my miracle because trying to hack your growth is detrimental. You will spend more time trying to growth hack or shortcut something then you would simply doing the process. Having a successful business or having your business get acquired as an entrepreneur is not like winning the golden ticket or the lottery. You have to work for it. If you don't do the work, you won't change in the process, and then you won't be who you need to be at the end to maintain and steward the miracle. Success is meant to be a process, so trying to hack it is a waste of time.

FARMING SUCCESS

I grew up on a farm in the South Carolina countryside, and farming was a large part of our community. As a kid, I watched the farmers diligently working, but one thing I never saw was a farmer standing in the middle of a field yelling at the ground to grow—trying to hack the process in some way. Instead, farmers commit to the process of preparing the soil, fertilizing it, planting seeds, tending the ground, protecting the budding plants from the elements and predators, and then working hard to bring in and store the harvest. The harvest is a byproduct of the process of farming. These farmers work hard, but their hard work always pays off. In the same way, there is no "Miracle Grow" for lasting success and growth. You can be efficient in your process, but growth is still a process. Since I'm using farming terms, fruit or success is always a byproduct of your process. You can't hack making fruit. Success and growth for your business is a byproduct of other processes you deployed.

COMMITMENT

For my company, growth is the byproduct of three processes I have put into place: commitment, culture, and courage. If I want to grow my bottom line, then my commitment process needs to be improved. This requires me to assess how appealing my company is to customers so I can increase the interest level. I also access what my conversion rates are, and are my customers making purchases at conversion. Am I getting repeat purchases? All of these connect back to commitment. I focus on my process and then I trust growth because the fruit will come.

> YOU CAN'T HACK GROWTH BECAUSE, FUNDAMENTALLY, GROWTH IS A BYPRODUCT.

If you have seeds in your hands and you sprayed them with fertilizer and yelled at them to grow, nothing will happen until you begin the process of planting them in the right environment. You have your process to do, but the seed has its process, too. The seed process happens in the nutrient rich soil, photosynthesis needs to take place, the seed will need water—all of this is part of the process the seed will experience. Your piece of the process is one part of a collective whole that is interdependent.

The way we connect this analogy of process to the business world is that your seed is your product. You have to place your product in the right environment, which is giving it to customers. Then you have to wait on the outside forces of sun and water, which represent product fit, affiliate marketing, product perception, and product value. The product value means your product will grow tall and have deep roots so it can withstand the storms without getting blown away. All the aspects of the process must take place for growth to happen. You can't hack growth because, fundamentally, growth is a byproduct.

CULTURE

In the same way you can't hack growth and so you need commitment, you can't hack the environment, which is why you will need to do the work of creating culture for your business or organization. In life, you will have to do two things: prepare or repair—but it is always more expensive to repair what you have broken. When the culture or the environment is broken, the CEO or leader will try to repair the culture. Maybe this sounds like, "To have culture we need to have five company outings a year and nine zoom meetings a month, and we're going to meet at the end of each day to hang out."

IF YOU TRY TO HACK THE ENVIRONMENT AND FAKE THE RELATIONSHIP, IT WILL BE OBVIOUS TO EVERYONE.

These steps are their attempt to repair a broken culture and hopefully build a new one. But there is no substitute for the process of building genuine relationships. You either have a relationship with your people or you don't. You can't fake it. If you try to hack the environment and fake the relationship, it will be obvious to everyone. You can't hack culture. It is more effective to proactively build and grow culture before it breaks. Like farming, to successfully grow your company's culture, you need to give it the nutrients of time, energy, attention, and encouragement. But you have to prepare the environment for the process. And this happens through open dialogue where you invite your employees to speak into the process of what you are wanting to achieve—a healthy company culture. If you don't let them know the strategy you are deploying then they may feel smothered in the process. So let them speak into what is most needed for them to build relationships within the organization.

COURAGE

Many business leaders want to hack the future, and get to the future results now. But this skips the process of how courage is developed in you as the leader. Courage requires you to face issues that will arise with the mindset that you can figure it out. If you skip this process, you will skip the opportunity for confidence to be planted in you. You can't hack confidence and courage. You have to go through the process of needing to be courageous because courage is a byproduct of facing your fears and not backing down.

With enough time, resources, and people around you, you can solve any problem. But you have to be willing to face today's problems and solve them. There is no hack for this, and you can't skip to the future. The process for your future results

YOU CAN'T GET TOMORROW'S RESULTS WITHOUT GOING THROUGH TODAY'S PROCESS.

are established and you have to let it play itself out while you maintain your process of farming. You can't get tomorrow's results without going through today's process.

Tomorrow's results are already there, but they are sitting in tomorrow. You can't bring them toward you. You have to wait for the process of time. Tomorrow's results are always going to be tomorrow's results. All you can do is work hard today so you can make tomorrow's results better. All you and I have is right now. Don't worry about yesterday's results because they are gone and you can't go back and fix them. But today, you have tomorrow's results in your hands, so do the next right thing now.

CHANGED BY THE PROCESS

If I became a billionaire overnight through the lottery, most likely I wouldn't be one for very long. Instant wins and lucky breaks show us the folly of a hacked system. I wouldn't know how to maintain that level of wealth because I didn't participate in a process that achieved it. Receiving a sudden harvest with no process ruins the outcome because you need to understand the work it took to get there so you can maintain the outcome. There is a saying that I live by in the corporate world: "A lack of understanding will always lead to abuse." For example, if I

A LACK OF UNDERSTANDING WILL ALWAYS LEAD TO ABUSE.

had an expensive phone, but I didn't understand its purpose, and instead of using it like a phone I used it like a hammer, the phone would be ruined because of my lack of understanding of what it was meant for. The phone would be destroyed because I didn't understand the intended purpose. Similarly, if I don't understand the purpose of wealth and success because I haven't walked through the process, then when I get these things, I will unintentionally abuse them.

You only learn the purpose and value of something through the process. Someone can tell you its purpose—the purpose of a healthy family, marriage, or successful business—but only in the process of being married, having a family, or running a business do I understand its purpose. I didn't understand finances until I had to run a business. I didn't understand success until I had to go after it. Taking part in the process made me understand the purpose of what mattered to me. I would never have a purpose without a process.

PLANTING HUMILITY

The law of planting and reaping is true, and at the end of the day, as you take your miracle into the world, I hope you plant goodness into the lives of others. If you have viewed business as being cutthroat, and so perhaps have made choices or planted seeds that weren't good into other people's soil, then go back and plant humility. Own your mistakes and apologize. You can plant a new seed in old dirt, and it will still grow a tree. The earth has been here for a long time, and people are always putting new seeds into old dirt and watching trees sprout. In the same way, you can have old experiences that weren't good, but you can go back and plant humility in them. By doing this, you can experience fruit in the present by planting seeds in the past. It's never too late.

MOVING FORWARD

As the movie fades, Jiminy begins to sing; about how nothing is too extreme to dream about. We all should dream big dreams because they will come true. You can start today executing toward your dream too. As leaders and entrepreneurs, it's your job to go somewhere worth going and to teach people how to follow you there. Stay on mission, and in the face of doubt, keep moving forward toward your dream. It is natural to doubt yourself, but what you do with it makes all the difference.

Never doubt that you are a miracle, but remember miracles never exist for themselves. Pinocchio is a tragedy because he didn't realize he was a miracle; instead he spends the entire story trying to marginalize himself—how tragic. You are a supernatural phenomenon, and normal isn't aspirational. Don't make the same mistake Pinocchio made by desiring to become "normal." Understanding the capacity for the miraculous inside of yourself is key to your success as an entrepreneur. But remember, miracles are never self-serving.

Commit yourself and your miracle to the process because there are no shortcuts to fully alive dreams. When outside forces bring their abilities to bear on your behalf, you will be ready because you will have planted the seeds and participated in the process. Your dream is worth the effort you will need to bring it to pass, so commit to the process and move forward. Plant today for tomorrow's success because dreams really do come true.

CITATIONS

[1] https://sourcesofinsight.com/lessons-learned-from-john-maxwell/

[2] Reiner, Rob, director. *The American President*. 1995.

[3] "Proverbs 11:14." *The Holy Bible: Containing the Old and New Testaments Translated out of the Original Tongues and with the Former Translations Diligently Compared & Revised*, American Bible Society, 1986.

[4] Disney, Walt, et al. *Pinocchio*.

Printed in the USA
CPSIA information can be obtained
at www.ICGtesting.com
JSHW041958020823
45733JS00004B/17